FACE-OFF!

Top 10 Lists of *Everything* in HOCKEY

Managing Editor, Sports Illustrated Kids **Mark Bechtel**

Creative Director **Beth Bugler**

Photo Editor **Claire Bourgeois**

Writer **Sarah Kwak**

Editors **Elizabeth McGarr McCue, Sam Page**

Copy Editor **Pamela Ann Roberts**

Designer **Kirsten Sorton**

Reporter **Lauren Shute**

Time Inc. Premedia **Geoffrey Michaud, Dan Larkin**

TIME INC. BOOKS

Publisher Margot Schupf
Vice President, Finance Terri Lombardi
Executive Director, Marketing Services Carol Pittard
Executive Director, Business Development Suzanne Albert
Executive Director, Marketing Susan Hettleman
Executive Publishing Director Megan Pearlman
Associate Director of Publicity Courtney Greenhalgh
Assistant General Counsel Simone Procas
Assistant Director, Special Sales Ilene Schreider
Assistant Director, Finance Christine Font
Assistant Production Director Susan Chodakiewicz
Senior Manager, Sales Marketing Danielle Costa
Senior Manager, Children's Category Marketing Amanda Lipnick
Manager, Business Development and Partnerships Stephanie Braga
Associate Prepress Manager Alex Voznesenskiy

***

Editorial Director Stephen Koepp
Art Director Gary Stewart
Senior Editors Roe D'Angelo, Alyssa Smith
Managing Editor Matt DeMazza
Editor, Children's Books Jonathan White
Copy Chief Rina Bander
Design Manager Anne-Michelle Gallero
Assistant Managing Editor Gina Scauzillo
Editorial Assistant Courtney Mifsud

***

Special thanks: Allyson Angle, Katherine Barnet, Brad Beatson, Jeremy Biloon, Ian Chin, Rose Cirrincione, Pat Datta, Assu Etsubneh, Alison Foster, Erika Hawxhurst, Kristina Jutzi, David Kahn, Jean Kennedy, Hillary Leary, Samantha Long, Amy Mangus, Kimberly Marshall, Robert Martells, Nina Mistry, Melissa Presti, Danielle Prielipp, Kate Roncinske, Babette Ross, Dave Rozzelle, Matthew Ryan, Ricardo Santiago, Divyam Shrivastava

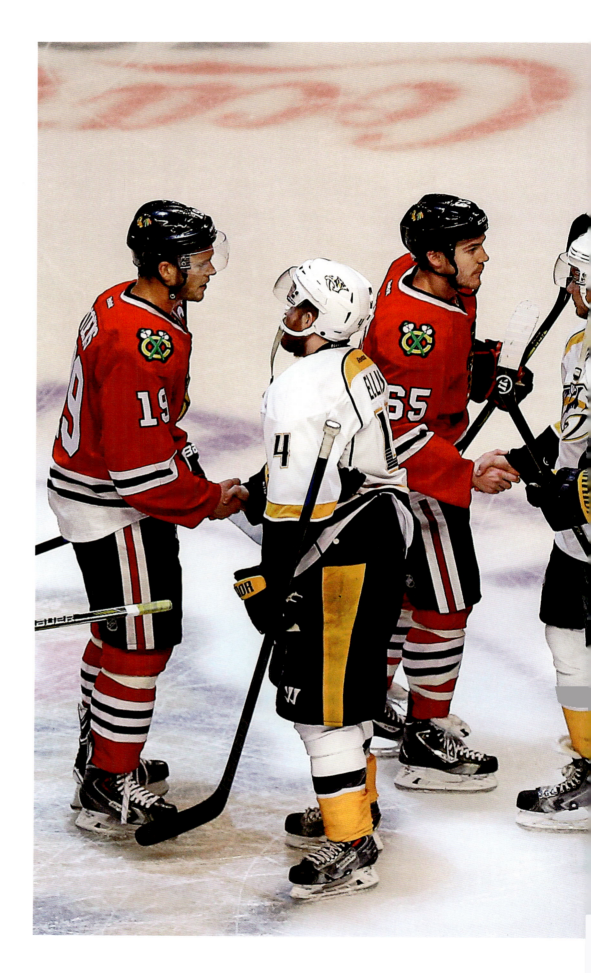

The handshake line at the conclusion of every postseason series is hockey's top tradition.

The Top 10 LISTS

When it comes to a shootout, few players find the net as often as Chicago Blackhawks captain Jonathan Toews.

TOP 10
GREATEST
PLAYERS

Wayne Gretzky

Born in Brantford, Ontario, Canada, Gretzky began building his legend at an early age. When he was six, he played on a team with 10-year-olds. At 10, his play drew crowds and people began calling him the Great Gretzky. By the time he was 13, he had already scored 1,000 competitive goals. By the time he turned pro as a 17-year-old, the expectations for him were huge.

Gretzky didn't just live up to them. He exceeded them.

When he retired, he had 894 NHL goals — 93 more than any other player. No one has come within 700 assists of his career mark of 1,963. He was the only player to have 200 points in a season, and he did it four times. When Gretzky was on top of his game — which was most of the time — he was unstoppable. During the 1983–84 season, he had a point in 51 straight games. (Over the course of his 20-year NHL career, his longest drought without a point was four games.) He won seven straight Art Ross Trophies as the league's top scorer, and he was named NHL MVP nine times.

The Great One's greatness went beyond individual accomplishments. He led the Edmonton Oilers to four Stanley Cups. And he nearly delivered one to Los Angeles in 1993, when he took the Kings to the finals.

When Gretzky retired from the game in April 1999 as a member of the New York Rangers, the hockey world knew it was losing a living legend. Before his last game, the NHL decreed that no other player would ever wear Gretzky's iconic number 99. Seven months later, he was inducted into the Hockey Hall of Fame, bypassing the usual three-year waiting period between retirement and Hall eligibility.

It was a fitting tribute to hockey's first mainstream superstar, the man who was not only the game's preeminent talent, but also its most important.

Bobby Orr

A two-time NHL scoring champ, the longtime Boston Bruins defenseman revolutionized his position. Before he came into the league, blueliners rarely left the point when their team had the puck. But Orr freely roamed the ice and led end-to-end rushes. He was the team's offensive catalyst, becoming the first defenseman to break 100 points, in 1969–70. (His 139 points the next season remain the NHL record for the position.) Though best known for his offense, Orr was a dogged defender. In 1970, when he was 22, he was the first NHL player to be named Sportsman of the Year by SPORTS ILLUSTRATED. Writer Jack Olsen proclaimed, "Bobby Orr is the greatest player ever to don skates. Not the greatest defenseman, the greatest player at either end of the ice."

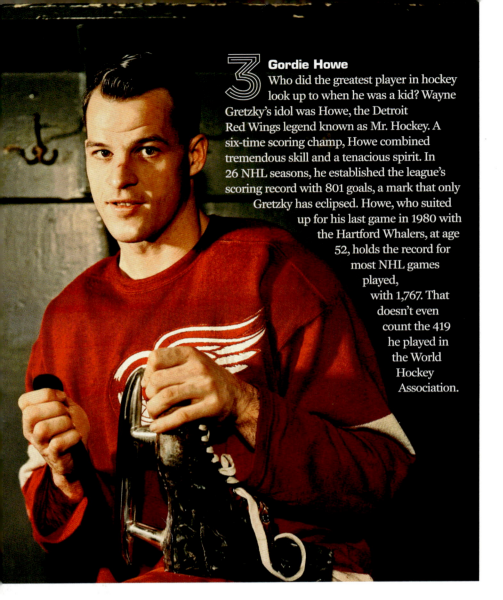

3 Gordie Howe

Who did the greatest player in hockey look up to when he was a kid? Wayne Gretzky's idol was Howe, the Detroit Red Wings legend known as Mr. Hockey. A six-time scoring champ, Howe combined tremendous skill and a tenacious spirit. In 26 NHL seasons, he established the league's scoring record with 801 goals, a mark that only Gretzky has eclipsed. Howe, who suited up for his last game in 1980 with the Hartford Whalers, at age 52, holds the record for most NHL games played, with 1,767. That doesn't even count the 419 he played in the World Hockey Association.

4 Mario Lemieux

A player with an impressive combination of size and skill, the 6'4", 230-pound Pittsburgh Penguins center made quite a first impression, scoring 100 points as a rookie in 1984–85. His long reach and solid frame made Lemieux nearly impossible to knock off the puck. Though often hampered by chronic health issues — a bad back and a bout with cancer — Lemieux still dominated the sport. He was limited to just 915 games, but he scored 1,723 points in his 17 seasons. His 1.88 points per game ranks second all time, behind only Gretzky.

7 Doug Harvey

Bobby Orr wasn't the only defenseman who played a critical role in his team's attack. Harvey was a key component to the Canadiens' Flying Frenchmen attack. His ability to fire off crisp outlet passes and manage the offense from the blue line set him apart from the defensemen of his era. Aside from his skill with the puck, Harvey was also a premier one-on-one defender. He was skilled enough with his stick to pickpocket any attacking player. When he retired in 1969, his 452 career assists were the best among defensemen and 10th overall. The pioneer of puck-moving defensemen, Harvey won the Norris Trophy, given to the top player at his position, seven times.

8 Bobby Hull

Few players can single-handedly change a game the way Hull could. With his quick acceleration and terrorizing shot, he was one of the most breathtaking players of the 1960s. Hull was the second-youngest player to win the scoring title when he had 39 goals and 42 assists in 1959–60, as a 21-year-old. A year later he brought the Stanley Cup to a Chicago Blackhawks franchise that had gone without a championship for 23 years. He became the first player to score more than 50 goals in a season, breaking the plateau in '65–66.

5 Maurice Richard
In the 1950s the Montreal Canadiens represented the best of the NHL. And Richard represented the best of the Canadiens. A fearsome scorer from the day his career began in 1942, he became the first player to score 50 goals in 50 games, in just his second full season in the league. But he may be best remembered for his fiery competitiveness on the ice. Facing the Boston Bruins in the '52 Stanley Cup semifinals, Richard scored the series-winner despite being knocked unconscious earlier in the game. In '98, the NHL established a trophy in his name, awarded to the league's leading goal scorer each year.

6 Jean Beliveau
A two-time MVP and the inaugural winner, in 1965, of the Conn Smythe Trophy as playoff MVP, the longtime Canadien was a role model and ambassador for the game. Known for his grace and class both on and off the ice, Beliveau scored 507 career goals and had 1,219 points. He was also the first hockey player to appear on the cover of SPORTS ILLUSTRATED, in January 1956.

9 Guy Lafleur
Three years after the Canadiens selected him first overall in the 1971 draft, Lafleur began a historic scoring run, becoming the first player to have at least 50 goals and 100 points for six straight seasons. That torrid pace helped Lafleur reach the 1,000-point mark in just his 720th game, faster than any player had done before. The speedy winger, who won five Stanley Cups with Montreal, led his team in scoring in eight of the 14 seasons he spent with the Canadiens. His 1,246 points remain a franchise record.

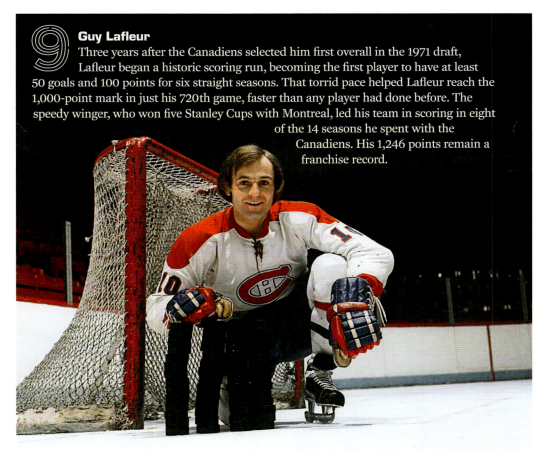

10 Patrick Roy
While leading two teams (the Canadiens and the Colorado Avalanche) to Stanley Cups and earning postseason MVP honors three times, Roy exemplified excellence under pressure. The career leader for playoff wins (151), Roy always performed best when the stakes were highest, and his form inspired a generation of goalies to play just like him.

Top 10 Trad

ditions

Handshake line

For decades, every NHL playoff series has ended the same way, with both teams looking past the on-ice battles and extending the enemy a cordial hand. The postseries handshake line is the most hallowed tradition in hockey. Its roots can be traced to the early 1900s, and within 20 years the handshake was a regular occurrence. It's not a rule that the teams shake hands. Rather, they line up out of respect for the game and for their opponents — no matter how contentious the series might have been. Says Brad Marchand of the Boston Bruins, "To show each other that respect at the end and realize that everything that's happened is just because we both want to win — it's definitely a great tradition."

2 Octopus on the ice at the Joe
What do octopi and hockey have to do with each other? Back during the league's Original Six days, a team had to win two four-games series to win the Stanley Cup. That meant it needed to win eight postseason games. So a couple of clever Red Wings fans thought that the octopus, with its eight legs, would nicely represent their team's quest for the Cup. For years, fans have smuggled raw octopi into Detroit's Joe Louis Arena and tossed them onto the ice. The responsibility of collecting the creatures is given to the Red Wings' longtime building manager and Zamboni driver, Al Sobotka. Before he leaves the ice, he often fires up the crowd by swinging an octopus above his head.

3 Chicago's national anthem
When national anthem singer Jim Cornelison strides out, the Chicago crowd begins to cheer. And it does not stop until he's done singing the "The Star-Spangled Banner." The practice started during the 1985 conference finals, when the Blackhawks met the mighty Oilers. After Edmonton outscored Chicago 18–5 in the first two games, Blackhawks fans took it upon themselves to fill the arena with energy before Game 3. Chicago won 5–2, and a tradition was born.

7 Stanley Cup day
In 1995, the NHL officially began giving each member of the Stanley Cup–winning team 24 hours with the trophy. Everyone from the president of the team to a third-line winger to the equipment manager gets a day to celebrate his or her part of the championship. As a result, the Cup has become perhaps the most traveled trophy in the world.

8 Don't touch the trophies
Athletes tend to be superstitious, but hockey players take the cake. Fearing a jinx, most players will not touch the Stanley Cup unless they've won it. And some refuse to touch the conference championship trophy — or even the table it rests on — because they view the Stanley Cup as the only trophy worth lifting. "It's saying we're here for bigger and better things," said Blackhawks captain Jonathan Toews in 2010.

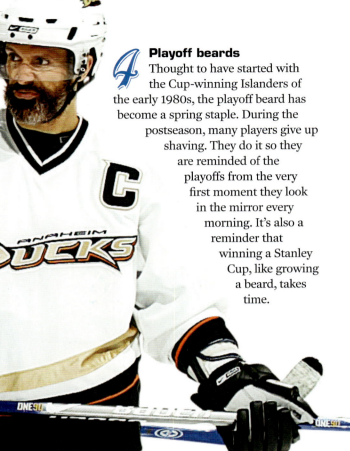

4 Playoff beards

Thought to have started with the Cup-winning Islanders of the early 1980s, the playoff beard has become a spring staple. During the postseason, many players give up shaving. They do it so they are reminded of the playoffs from the very first moment they look in the mirror every morning. It's also a reminder that winning a Stanley Cup, like growing a beard, takes time.

5 Hats on the ice for a hat trick

The hat trick grew in popularity in the 1940s, when legend has it a Toronto hat maker promised a free lid to Maple Leafs players who scored three goals in a game. Now fans celebrate hat tricks by throwing their hats onto the ice. Where do all the hats go? Some teams give them to the player, some pile them into a display case in the arena, while others donate them to charity.

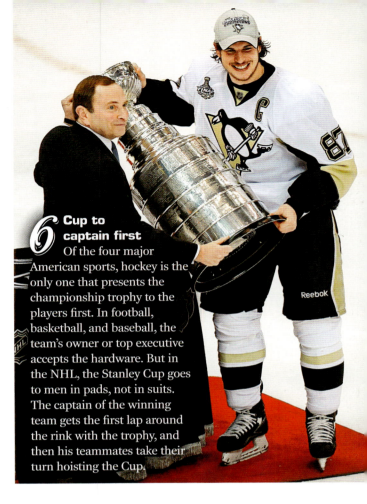

6 Cup to captain first

Of the four major American sports, hockey is the only one that presents the championship trophy to the players first. In football, basketball, and baseball, the team's owner or top executive accepts the hardware. But in the NHL, the Stanley Cup goes to men in pads, not in suits. The captain of the winning team gets the first lap around the rink with the trophy, and then his teammates take their turn hoisting the Cup.

9 "God Bless America," by Kate Smith

In the late 1960s the Philadelphia Flyers began occasionally playing a recording of Kate Smith singing "God Bless America" before games in place of the national anthem. Philadelphia seemed to play better with the new song. So when the Flyers had a chance to wrap up their first Stanley Cup in 1974, they brought in Smith to sing before Game 6 of the finals. They won, and the recording of that performance is still shown on the video screen before some Philadelphia games.

10 Winter Classic

The NHL took the idea of outdoor hockey and turned it into a spectacle. On New Year's Day 2008, Sidney Crosby and the Pittsburgh Penguins beat the Buffalo Sabres in a snowy shootout at Ralph Wilson Stadium. That began an annual tradition of bringing hockey to iconic outdoor venues like Fenway Park in Boston and Michigan Stadium in Ann Arbor. The NHL's Winter Classic blends history with technology, resulting in an unforgettable show.

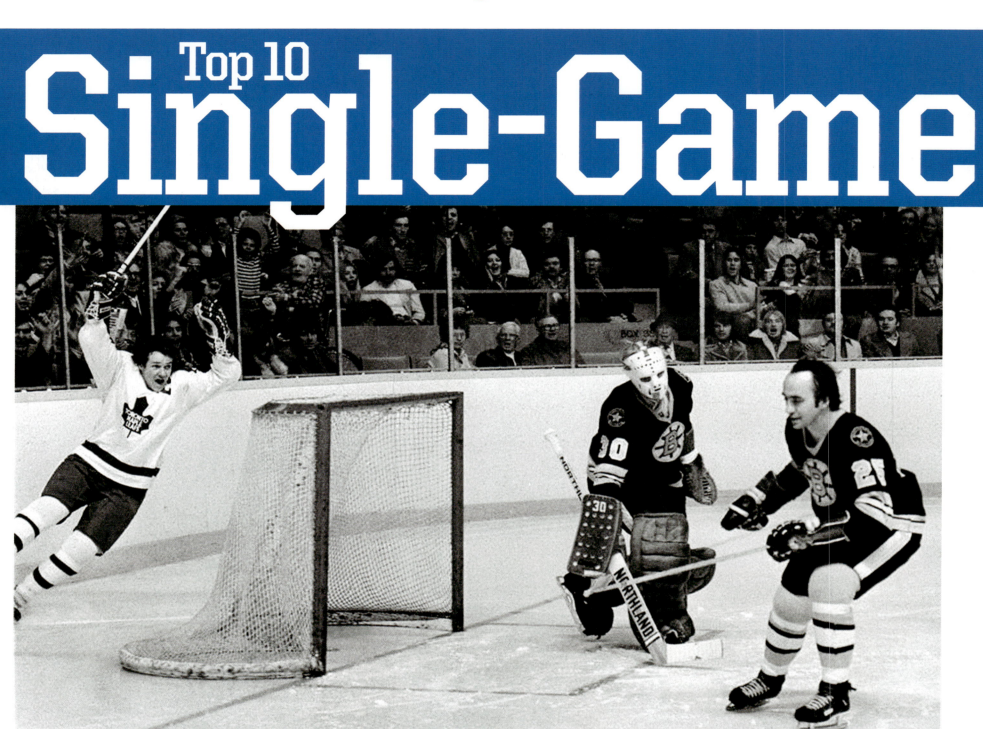

Top 10
Single-Game

1 Darryl Sittler, February 7, 1976

On a Saturday night at Maple Leaf Gardens, Toronto captain Darryl Sittler had 10 points in one game, setting a magical record that has never been topped. Heading into the match, the Boston Bruins were riding a seven-game winning streak. But with their regular goalie, Gilles Gilbert, injured, they started rookie Dave Reece. The Maple Leafs took advantage, scoring twice in the first period, with Sittler assisting on both. Then the center went on a tear, scoring hat tricks in both the second and third periods. He had a hand in all but one of Toronto's goals in the 11–4 rout.

Performances

2 Dominik Hasek, April 27, 1994
With his Buffalo Sabres facing elimination in Game 6 of their first-round series against the New Jersey Devils, Hasek won a goaltender's duel with Martin Brodeur. Neither team scored until Buffalo center Dave Hannan broke through in the fourth overtime. Hasek finished with 70 saves in his second shutout of the series.

3 Sidney Crosby, November 21, 2011
In January 2011, the Pittsburgh Penguins' captain suffered a severe concussion that sidelined him for more than 10 months. His prolonged absence led many to wonder if the 24-year-old superstar would be the same player when he returned. In his first game back in Pittsburgh, he erased any doubt, scoring on his first shot and finishing the night with four points in the Penguins' 5–0 win over the New York Islanders.

4 Mario Lemieux, December 31, 1988
In an 8–6 win over the New Jersey Devils, Super Mario did something no one had ever done before or has done since. He scored goals in five different ways: at even strength, on the power play, shorthanded, on a penalty shot, and into an empty net. His first goal came 4:17 into the game, and he shot home the empty netter with just one second remaining.

5 T.J. Oshie, February 15, 2014
In Team USA's preliminary-round game against Russia at the 2014 Olympics, U.S. winger Oshie was limited to just 15 shifts and less than 10 minutes of ice time. But after the final horn sounded, Oshie put on a dazzling performance, going 4 for 6 in an eight-round shootout to win the game for Team USA.

6 Joe Malone, January 31, 1920
Playing for the Quebec Bulldogs in the third season of the NHL, the center from Quebec City scored seven goals in his hometown team's 10–6 win over the Toronto St. Patricks. In the 95 years since, no NHL player has ever matched Malone's mark.

7 Al Hill, February 14, 1977
Beset by injuries to their star forwards, the Philadelphia Flyers called up Hill from the minors for a February game against the St. Louis Blues. Hill, a versatile 22-year-old, took the opportunity to set an NHL record by scoring five points (two goals, three assists) in his NHL debut.

8 Jeff Reese, February 10, 1993
While making 26 saves in a 13–1 blowout of the San Jose Sharks, the Calgary Flames goalie also became the first netminder to be credited with three assists in one game. In his other 173 career games, Reese had five assists.

9 Sam Gagner, February 2, 2012
In an 8–4 win over the Chicago Blackhawks, the Edmonton Oilers center became the first player in nearly 24 years to register eight points in one game. He had just five goals on the season going into the game, but he nearly doubled that total by adding four. It was the rare bright spot in Edmonton's otherwise lackluster season; the Oilers went on to finish last in their division for the third straight year.

10 Ian Turnbull, February 2, 1977
Who is the only defenseman to score more than four goals in a game? Not Hall of Famer Paul Coffey or Boston Bruins legend Bobby Orr. No, it was Turnbull, who netted five for the Toronto Maple Leafs in a win over the Detroit Red Wings.

TOP 10 RIVALRIES

Boston Bruins–Montreal Canadiens

The most familiar of foes, these two Original Six squads have faced each other 729 times during the regular season over 91 years, more than any other two teams in the NHL. In the postseason, Montreal holds a 106–71 advantage, which includes 18 straight series wins from 1946 to '87. More recently the rivalry has been more competitive, with Boston winning two of the last three. The meetings, always hard-fought and physical affairs, have been among the most memorable in hockey. In 1979 the Bruins were sunk by an infamous penalty for having too many men on the ice late in Game 7 of the semifinals. And in a meeting in 2011, the nastiness of the rivalry returned after Boston defenseman Zdeno Chara violently checked winger Max Pacioretty into a turnbuckle along the boards. The incident loomed over their first-round series that spring, when the Bruins overcame an 0–2 deficit to take the series in seven games.

2 Detroit Red Wings–Chicago Blackhawks
Seven years after joining the NHL the Red Wings and the Blackhawks faced off in the 1934 Stanley Cup finals. Chicago won the best-of-five series on a double-overtime goal in Game 4, but Detroit went on to win seven championships in the next 21 years. Their meetings have become less frequent since Detroit moved to the Eastern Conference in 2013, but die-hard fans can now hope for another Wings-Hawks final one day.

3 Montreal Canadiens–Toronto Maple Leafs
Toronto calls itself the Center of the Hockey Universe, while Montreal likens its fervor for the Canadiens to a religion. Either way, the Canadian cities hold arguably the most ardent fan bases in the NHL. The meetings between the two oldest franchises are always intense, even if they seldom play each other in the postseason.

Toronto and Montreal have met in the playoffs just 15 times. In their last meeting, the 1979 quarterfinals, the Canadiens swept Toronto for the second straight year. Although the Leafs haven't enjoyed much success in recent years, failing to make the playoffs nine of the last 10 seasons, they have still managed a 29-21-12 record against their bitter rivals during that span.

4 Detroit Red Wings–Colorado Avalanche
Beginning in 1996, it seemed that each postseason featured a showdown between the two Western Conference powers. The Avalanche, led by goalie Patrick Roy, faced Steve Yzerman's Red Wings five times in seven years; three of those meetings came in the conference finals. But the rivalry was just as intense during the

regular season. The most notorious meeting between the clubs came on March 26, 1997, when the Wings and the Avalanche combined for 18 fighting majors. Detroit won that game 6–5 in overtime. The Red Wings prevailed again in the playoffs later that year on their way to winning the the Stanley Cup. From '96 through 2002, Detroit and Colorado combined to win all but two Cup titles.

5 Edmonton Oilers–Calgary Flames

In 1980, a year after the Oilers joined the NHL from the World Hockey Association, the Atlanta Flames moved north and west, to Calgary. So began the Battle of Alberta, the Canadian province that is home to both teams. From 1983

to '90, either the Flames or the Oilers were playing in the Stanley Cup finals. Edmonton, with a roster loaded with Hall of Famers, won five Cups during that span, while the Flames won in '89, their only championship to date. The rivalry has cooled in recent years — the teams last met in the playoffs in '91. They even became trade partners for the first time in 2010.

6 Philadelphia Flyers–Pittsburgh Penguins

Both franchises joined the NHL in 1967, but there was not much of a rivalry in the early days. The Flyers had built themselves into Stanley Cup winners by 1974, while Pittsburgh struggled to put together winning seasons. Philadelphia

essentially dominated the meetings, going 59-24-16 through 1983–84. But then the Penguins drafted Mario Lemieux, and the Keystone State rivalry began to flourish. It hit a fever pitch after Penguins center Sidney Crosby emerged as the face of the league. Since 2007 the teams have met in the playoffs three times, with Pittsburgh prevailing twice.

7 New York Rangers–New York Islanders

The two franchises were separated by just 28 miles, but they felt a world apart. The Islanders, out of suburban Uniondale, long lived in the shadows of the metropolitan Rangers, who play in the middle of Manhattan. Even when they

won four straight Stanley Cups in the 1980s, the Islanders never seemed to gain the mainstream following the Rangers enjoyed. The teams haven't met in the postseason in more than 20 years. But with the Islanders moving to Brooklyn and both teams enjoying regular-season success, an interborough series could soon be on the horizon.

8 Montreal Canadiens–Quebec Nordiques

For 16 seasons, from 1979–80 through '94–95, Quebec was divided between the old-guard Canadiens and the Nordiques, who came from the WHA. A thrilling series in '82, which Quebec won in overtime of a do-or-die Game 5, set the tone for a

memorable matchup two years later. Montreal held a 3–2 series advantage when, in Game 6, the animosity between the teams boiled over. A bench-clearing brawl broke out in the second period, and then another occurred after the period ended. Ten players were ejected as the teams were assessed more than 250 penalty minutes. And by the way, the Canadiens won the game 5–3.

9 U.S.S.R.–Canada

Canada may be hockey's home, but in the 1970s and '80s, the Soviet Union made a huge impact on the game in North America. With their graceful play and puck-possession style, the Soviets first took Canada by surprise in the 1972

Summit Series, building a 3-1-1 lead going into Game 6. But Team Canada pulled off an epic comeback, winning the last three games — all on the road. Canada has had numerous showdowns with the Soviet Union (and later, Russia) in the years since. Occasionally it's been a nasty rivalry: At the 1987 World Juniors, both teams were kicked out after a massive brawl.

10 U.S.A.–Canada women

Since 1990, when the first women's world championship took place, the United States and Canada have met in nearly every meaningful gold medal match. They've met in 16 world championships (10–6 in favor of Canada) and four

Olympics (3–1 to Canada). And each high-stakes meeting seems to produce a game more thrilling than the last. At the 2014 Olympic gold medal game, Team Canada came back from two goals down in the last four minutes of regulation to force overtime. Winger Marie-Philip Poulin scored in the extra period, denying the U.S. its first gold since 1998.

TOP SMI

1 Bobby Clarke
The Flyers' captain during Philadelphia's Broad Street Bullies days, Clarke personified the team's tenacity and aggressiveness. Letting nothing slow him down, he set the franchise record with 1,210 career points, and he led Philadelphia to Stanley Cups in 1974 and '75 — the team's only titles.

2 Alex Ovechkin
The Washington Capitals captain has had plenty to grin about: an Art Ross Trophy (scoring champ), three Harts (MVP), five Richards (most goals) and a Calder (rookie of the year). One thing that has eluded the ace scorer, however, is a Stanley Cup.

3 Bobby Hull
His exciting end-to-end rushes got Chicago Blackhawks fans out of their seats for 15 years. And his blazing, accurate shot helped him net 610 career goals, which was second only to Gordie Howe when Hull retired in 1980.

4 Daniel Carcillo
One of the league's most notorious fighters, he plays with an edge that at times goes too far. He has been fined or suspended 12 times in his career. Though the winger has never scored more than 13 goals in a season, his grit has made him a valuable asset on five different teams over the past nine seasons.

5 Matthew Barnaby
During a Buffalo Sabres playoff run in 1997, the on-ice pest had six of his teeth knocked out in a game. As a quick fix, Barnaby had partial dentures made that featured two silver front teeth. One had the Sabres' logo carved into it, and the other had his number, 36.

6 Ken Daneyko
The rugged, hard-hitting Devils defenseman has sacrificed plenty for the sake of Stanley Cup glory. On his way to winning three championships over 20 years with New Jersey, Daneyko lost 12 of his front teeth: five upper and seven lower.

10 LES

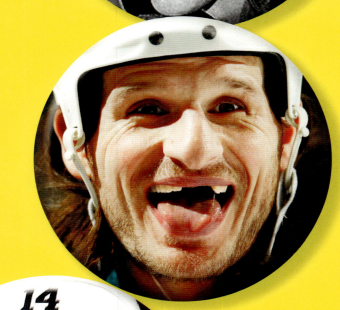

7 Duncan Keith

During Game 4 of the 2010 Western Conference finals, the Blackhawks defenseman took a shot square to the mouth and spit out seven of his teeth. He returned to the game seven minutes later, getting an assist to help Chicago advance to the Stanley Cup finals. Keith was all smiles three weeks later, as the Blackhawks celebrated their first Cup in 49 years.

8 Sean Couturier

Any Flyers draft pick would love to be compared favorably with the player at the top of this list. Well, Couturier certainly is reminiscent of Bobby Clarke when it comes to his teeth. (Or lack of them.) Philadelphia's 2011 first-round pick lost several of his top front teeth as a junior player before the draft, meaning he entered the NHL with a Clarke-like grin. On the ice, however, Couturier has a ways to go to challenge his toothless predecessor.

9 Mike Ricci

The fourth pick in the 1990 draft, Ricci sported a unique look on the ice with his long dark hair, an oft-broken nose, and an ever-present gap-tooth grin. He enjoyed a long career, breaking the 20-goal plateau six times over 16 NHL seasons.

10 Gordie Howe

It's impossible to leave Mr. Hockey off a list of hockey smiles. After all, in his very first NHL game, in 1946, he scored a goal and lost three teeth. Supremely skilled and tough as nails, Howe went on to play in the NHL for 25 more seasons, last suiting up for the Hartford Whalers at age 52.

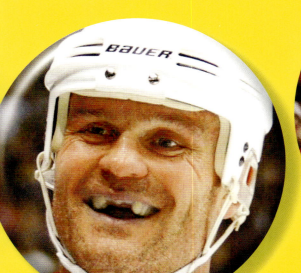

1 **Pavel Bure**
He earned the nickname Russian Rocket for his soaring speed and scoring touch. By 24, Bure already had two 60-goal seasons. When he went one-on-one with a defenseman, Bure blew past his man more often than not.

2 **Sergei Fedorov**
Though perhaps not the most explosive skater, Fedorov's stride gave him top-end speed. He won the first Fastest Skater competition at the 1992 All-Star weekend. And his maneuverability made him impossible to catch.

3 **Mike Gartner**
A speed demon well into his 30s, Gartner used his legs to become one of the most consistent goal scorers of his generation. In 19 seasons with five teams, Gartner scored 30 or more goals 17 times.

4 **Carl Hagelin**
The swift Swede is often just a blur on the ice. A hockey technology company measured the New York Rangers winger's top speed at 23 miles per hour in 2014, which made him the fastest player in the NHL.

5 **Yvan Cournoyer**
To make up for his relatively small size, Cournoyer could skate like the wind. His blazing speed kept him in the NHL for 16 seasons (all with the Montreal Canadiens) and earned him the nickname the Roadrunner.

Top 10 FASTEST

6 **Michael Grabner**
In his first season with the New York Islanders, in 2010–11, Grabner stormed his way to 34 goals. But he uses his speed on both sides of the puck; he has turned himself into one of the Islanders' top penalty killers.

7 **Bobby Orr**
The legendary Boston Bruins defenseman was famous for his spectacular end-to-end rushes. How was Orr able to carry the puck so far? Well, because he was fast and elusive, weaving through opponents with ease.

8 **Bobby Hull**
Once clocked on the ice at 29.7 miles per hour, the Golden Jet possessed incredible breakaway speed, which gave the Chicago Blackhawks icon the time and space to unleash his signature wicked slap shot.

9 **Nathan MacKinnon**
The 2013–14 rookie of the year showed how fast he was just before the beginning of his second season by racing — and beating — a three-time Olympic gold-medal-winning short track speedskater.

10 **Howie Morenz**
The first player to have his number retired by the Canadiens, Morenz dazzled during the early days of the NHL. Known as the Stratford Streak and the Mitchell Meteor, Morenz was the fastest skater of his day.

SKATERS

TOP 10
LITTLE GUYS

Height: 5'8" Weight: 180

1 Martin St. Louis
St. Louis was a four-year standout at the University of Vermont. He was a three-time finalist for the Hobey Baker Award, which is given to the top college player. Still, the winger went unsigned by an NHL team for nearly a year after graduation. His breakout season came in 2003–04, when he led the Tampa Bay Lightning to the Stanley Cup. That season he led the league in scoring and won the Hart Trophy as the NHL's MVP. His size never held him back, and neither has his age. In the shortened 2012–13 season, he again led the league with 60 points — when he was 37.

Height: 5'7" Weight: 172

4 Yvan Cournoyer
What the right winger lacked in size, he made up for in speed. Deceptively strong on his skates, the ever-confident Cournoyer took pleasure in proving his skeptics wrong. "I remember a coach telling me I looked too small to play on his team," Cournoyer once said. "All I said to to him was, 'Try me.'" In 16 seasons with the Canadiens, Cournoyer won 10 Stanley Cups, scored 428 goals, and earned a Conn Smythe Trophy as the MVP of the playoffs in 1973.

Height: 5'7" Weight: 160

2 Henri Richard
He grew up — both figuratively and literally — in the long shadow of his older brother Maurice, one of the best players in NHL history. But that never deterred Henri. Fourteen years younger and three inches shorter, Henri used his brother's legacy as motivation and eventually joined him on the Montreal Canadiens roster in 1955. They went on to win five straight Cups together before Maurice retired in 1960. Without his older brother, Henri still went on to carve out his own place in Canadiens history. With 1,046 points over 20 seasons, he ranks third in career scoring for the storied franchise.

Height: 5'6" Weight: 182

3 Theo Fleury
Playing in an era when big bodies ruled the NHL, Fleury never shied from using a physical game. He is one of 33 players to amass at least 1,000 points and penalty minutes. (Fleury had 1,088 points and 1,840 penalty minutes.) He would say his small stature even helped him win a Stanley Cup (in 1989 with the Calgary Flames) and an Olympic gold medal (in 2002 with Canada).

Height: 5'8" Weight: 185

5 Marcel Dionne
Drafted second overall in 1971 behind the legendary Guy Lafleur, the Little Beaver played four seasons for an underwhelming Detroit Red Wings team before heading west and joining the Los Angeles Kings. In L.A., he became the franchise's first star. But playing all the way out in California, Dionne often was overlooked; he never won a Hart Trophy, despite finishing in the top two in scoring four times.

Height: 5'7" Weight: 180

8 Gump Worsley
After winning the Calder Trophy for rookie of the year with the second-rate New York Rangers in 1952–53, Worsley had to wait 12 years before playing for a Stanley Cup winner. Traded to Montreal in 1963, Worsley went on to win four Cups with the dominant Canadiens of the '60s. The Hall of Famer still holds the best postseason win percentage (.806) in franchise history.

Height: 5'9" Weight: 190

9 Pat Verbeek
His Rangers teammate Glenn Healy dubbed the right winger Little Ball of Hate for Verbeek's aggressiveness on the ice and his compact frame. Playing for five teams over a 20-year career, Verbeek scored 522 career goals. That's impressive considering he also served 2,905 penalty minutes in the 1,424 games he played.

Height: 5'8" Weight: 163

6 Ted Lindsay
He earned his nickname Terrible Ted for his mean streak on the ice, holding the record for career penalty minutes for 18 years. But Lindsay was a multidimensional threat, stringing together eight straight seasons with 20 or more goals. He regularly held his own against much larger opponents on the ice, and as an early pioneer of the NHL Players' Association, Lindsay could certainly put up a fight.

Height: 5'3" Weight: 135

7 Roy Worters
Nicknamed Shrimp, Worters was the smallest player in NHL history. He played 12 seasons during the earliest days of the league. Aside from one game he played with the Canadiens in 1930, Worters suited up with the now-defunct Pittsburgh Pirates and New York Americans from 1925 to 1937. He was the first goalie to win the Hart Trophy. His 67 shutouts still rank 14th all-time, but he never won a Stanley Cup.

Height: 5'7" Weight: 176

10 Brian Gionta
In four years with Boston College, which culminated in an NCAA championship in 2001, the undersized winger developed his own brand of high-energy, hard-working hockey. Drafted in the third round by the New Jersey Devils in 1998, he was instrumental in the team's Stanley Cup win in 2003, just his second NHL season. Later in his career, he became known for his leadership qualities, serving as captain of the Canadiens and the Buffalo Sabres.

BIG GUYS

Height: 6'9"   Weight: 255

Height: 6'3"   Weight: 205

Height: 6'4"   Weight: 230

Height: 6'5"   Weight: 210

Height: 6'6"   Weight: 220

1 Zdeno Chara
The Boston Bruins' captain is the tallest player in NHL history. On skates, Chara approaches the 7-foot mark. His exceptionally long stick is two inches taller than NHL rules usually allow, but because of his height, Chara has special permission to use it.

2 Jean Beliveau
Nicknamed *Le Gros Bill* (French for Big Bill), Beliveau was known in Montreal as the Canadiens' gentle giant through the 1950s and '60s. A classy and elegant skater, he won the first-ever Conn Smythe Trophy as the playoff MVP in 1965.

3 Mario Lemieux
Four inches taller and 45 pounds heavier than Wayne Gretzky, Lemieux possessed a remarkable combination of size, strength, and skill. His balance and reach made him a dominating presence — and a threat everywhere on the ice.

4 Pete Mahovlich
Though he was known as Little M, there wasn't much small about Mahovlich. (His brother was Big M.) He won four Stanley Cups with the Canadiens in the 1970s and had consecutive 100-point seasons when he centered legends Guy Lafleur and Steve Shutt.

5 Chris Pronger
The defenseman's size and his mean streak made him one of the most intimidating players of his day. Success seemed to follow him. From 2005 to '10, Pronger took three teams to the finals, winning with the Anaheim Ducks in '07.

| Height: 6'3" | Weight: 215 | Height: 6'4" | Weight: 220 | Height: 6'5" | Weight: 231 | Height: 6'4" | Weight: 240 | Height: 6'5" | Weight: 260 |

6 Clark Gillies
The winger from the town of Moose Jaw, Saskatchewan, was a perfect combination of toughness and skill. Never afraid to throw around his body to make a play, he was the prototypical power forward of the 1970s and '80s with the New York Islanders.

7 Joe Thornton
Nicknamed Jumbo, the laid-back center led the league in assists for three straight seasons. Thornton was also the only player to be traded during an MVP season, winning the Hart Trophy in 2006 when he was sent from the Boston Bruins to the San Jose Sharks.

8 Mats Sundin
Though he never won a Stanley Cup, the Toronto Maple Leafs center was inducted into the Hall of Fame in 2012. Sundin had at least 70 points in 15 consecutive seasons (not counting the lockout-shortened 1994–95 season).

9 Eric Lindros
Drafted first overall by the Quebec Nordiques in 1991, the winger was immediately traded to Philadelphia. Lindros led the Flyers to the 1997 Stanley Cup finals and later starred for the New York Rangers. His career was cut short by concussions.

10 Dustin Byfuglien
Built like a linebacker, the Winnipeg Jets defenseman has been a contributor on both ends of the ice. He has scored 20 goals twice and finished in the top five in scoring for defensemen three times since joining the Jets in 2010.

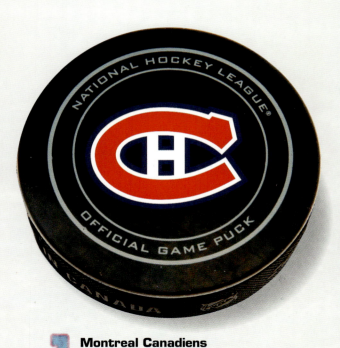

3 **Detroit Red Wings**
After six mostly unsuccessful seasons as the Cougars and then the Falcons, Detroit's hockey club became the Red Wings in 1932. The winged-wheel logo was a perfect symbol for the team from the Motor City, as Detroit is known because of its association with the car industry.

2 **Chicago Blackhawks**
Founding owner Major Frederic McLaughlin named his team after the Army regiment he commanded during World War I. His Black Hawk Division took its name from the Sauk Indian chief Black Hawk, who serves as the inspiration for the Native American head that adorns Chicago's sweaters.

1 **Montreal Canadiens**
As iconic and enduring as the New York Yankees' interlocking NY, Montreal's CH has been part of the team's logo since as far back as 1916. Contrary to popular lore, though, the H does not stand for *les Habitants*, or Habs, as the team is often called by locals. No, the H was adopted when the team was fully renamed *Le club de Hockey Canadien* in 1916. The H, therefore, stands for hockey.

Top 10 Logos

6 **Boston Bruins**
The spoked B logo was introduced in 1948, inspired by the idea that Boston is "the hub of the solar system," as 19th century poet Oliver Wendell Holmes once said. With a B at the center of the wheel, or at the hub, the logo represents the city that is home to the Bruins and a handful of successful college hockey teams, making Boston the Hub of Hockey.

7 **Philadelphia Flyers**
Names such as Liberty Bells and Quakers actually got more votes in a contest to choose the expansion team's name in 1966. But those names did not convey motion or excitement, so the team went with Flyers — and got a logo to match. The dynamic flying P has gone unchanged throughout the team's 48-year history.

Hartford Whalers
One of the four World Hockey Association teams absorbed into the NHL in 1979, the Whalers featured a logo that combined a W with a whale's tail. If you look closely, the space in between is in the shape of an H, for Hartford. Sadly, the logo isn't around any longer: The team moved to North Carolina in 1997.

Toronto Maple Leafs
When World War I veteran Conn Smythe bought a stake in the Toronto St. Pat's in 1927, he immediately renamed the team after Canada's national symbol: the maple leaf. The team's colors were also changed to blue (representing the country's blue skies) and white (snow). Though other cities may now protest, for many generations Toronto was considered Canada's team.

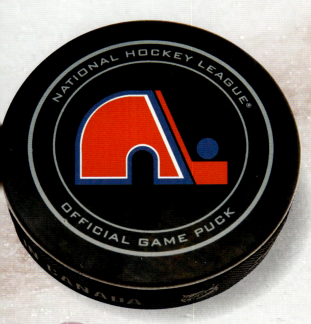

Quebec Nordiques
The Nordiques retained their WHA logo when they moved to the NHL in 1979. The igloo with a hockey stick represented the fact that the team played in the northernmost city — and one of the coldest — in the league.

New York Rangers
When Madison Square Garden president Tex Rickard was assembling a team to play at his arena back in 1926, the New York sportswriters began informally calling them "Tex's Rangers." The name stuck. Instead of going with a cowboy theme, they used a simple shield for their logo — a timeless symbol of strength and protection.

St. Louis Blues
Upon getting a franchise in St. Louis, Sid Salomon, the team's first owner, knew immediately that he wanted to name the team the Blues after a famous song from 1914. (It also honored the city's rich tradition of blues singers.) To go with the musical name, the team used a winged musical note as its logo.

G SERIES

1 Zdeno Chara

When the towering Boston Bruins captain winds up for a slap shot from the point, opposing players take notice — and take cover. With 255 pounds of power behind him, Chara has a cannon of a shot that is hard enough to do serious damage. In April 2011, for instance, one of his shots broke New York Rangers winger Ryan Callahan's leg. Chara has won the Hardest Shot contest at the NHL Super Skills competition five times, most recently in 2012, when he fired a puck a record 108.8 mph.

2 Al Iafrate

In 1993, Iafrate's shot at the Super Skills clocked in at 105.2 mph. That figure is made more impressive by the fact that he did it using a wooden stick and not the lighter composite models players use today.

6 Sergei Fedorov

The longtime Detroit Red Wings center is one of only two forwards to win the Hardest Shot competition. And he did it at age 32, when he was presumably past his physical peak.

TOP 10 HARDEST SHOTS

3 Shea Weber

How hard is Weber's shot? Well, the Nashville Predators' captain actually fired a puck through the net while playing for Team Canada at the 2010 Olympic Games. He nearly reached Chara's record mark, hitting 108.5 mph in 2015.

4 Al MacInnis

As a boy growing up in Nova Scotia, the Hall of Famer used to shoot pucks at a piece of plywood until blisters formed on his hands. All that practice paid off. MacInnis scored 340 goals in his 23-year career, the third most by a defenseman in NHL history.

5 Bobby Hull

Legend has it that one of Hull's slap shots topped 118 mph. His lightning-quick wrist shots were just as dangerous: The Golden Jet led the NHL in goals seven times (and the WHA once).

7 Bernie Geoffrion

Geoffrion claimed he invented the slap shot. That may or may not be true, but there's no arguing that the man nicknamed Boom Boom had one of the hardest shots of his day.

8 Adrian Aucoin

The big defenseman used his strong shot most effectively on the power play. Aucoin has scored almost half of his career goals when his team had a man advantage.

9 Steven Stamkos

The Tampa Bay Lightning center has a blistering one-timer. Thanks to that powerful shot, he led the league with 51 goals in the 2009–10 season, when he was just 19 years old.

10 Andy Bathgate

The winger had a mean slap shot, but his backhander was dangerous too. One of his shots cut Jacques Plante in 1959, leading to the debut of the goalie mask.

1 May 10, 1970: Bobby Orr Soars

With the Boston Bruins holding a 3–0 series lead over the St. Louis Blues in the Stanley Cup finals, the teams went to overtime in Game 4 at the famed Boston Garden. The extra frame lasted just 40 seconds, ending with one of the most memorable goals in NHL history. Driving hard to the net, Orr took a pass back from teammate Derek Sanderson and scored the Cup clincher. The goal, Orr's first of the finals, earned Boston its first Stanley Cup in 29 years. But more enduring than the play was the photo taken just after the puck hit the twine. Orr jumped in celebration (aided by Blues defenseman Noel Picard's stick), and for a moment, forever frozen on film, he flew.

2 April 10, 1982: Miracle on Manchester

In the NHL playoffs, no lead is safe. Just look at what happened in Game 3 of the first-round series between the Los Angeles Kings and the Edmonton Oilers in 1982. Playing on their home ice — the Forum, which was located on West Manchester Boulevard — the Kings fell behind 5–0. They still trailed by that score early in the third period, but then they scored five straight goals, the last coming with five seconds left, to tie the game. Winger Daryl Evans netted the winner 2:35 into overtime, giving Los Angeles a shocking win. The Kings went on to win the best-of-five series 3–2, knocking out the heavily favored Oilers.

TOP 10
OVERTIME GAMES

7 **March 24-25, 1936: The Marathon Game**
In Game 1 of their best-of-five series, the Montreal Maroons and the Red Wings played in what remains to this day the NHL's longest game. After a scoreless 176 minutes of hockey, Red Wings rookie Mud Bruneteau finally scored in the game's sixth overtime.

8 **June 19, 1999: Paint-gate**
Nearly 15 minutes into the third overtime of Game 6 of the Stanley Cup finals, Stars winger Brett Hull knocked in a rebound to win Dallas its first championship. One issue: Replays showed that part of Hull's skate was in the Buffalo crease. The goal stood — and it's still a sensitive subject for Sabres fans.

9 **April 23, 1950: Do-or-Die Sudden Death**
Sixteen Stanley Cup finals series have gone to Game 7; only two of those matches have gone into overtime. Talk about pressure. The first was in 1950, when the Red Wings and the Rangers played to a 3–3 tie. The winning goal finally came in the second OT, when Detroit's Pete Babando found the back of the Rangers' net.

10 **June 3, 1993: Stick-gate**
The Kings were on the verge of taking a commanding 2–0 lead over Montreal in the '93 finals. But with less than two minutes left in the game, Canadiens coach Jacques Demers asked referees to check L.A. winger Marty McSorley's stick. They did, and his stick was found to have too much curve. With McSorley in the penalty box, Montreal scored a power-play goal to tie the game, then won it 51 seconds into overtime.

3 **May 27, 1994: Matteau!**
With a trip to the Stanley Cup finals on the line, the New York Rangers broke a 1–1 tie against the New Jersey Devils early in the second overtime of Game 7 with a goal from Stephane Matteau. Just as memorable was announcer Howie Rose's call of the goal, screaming Matteau's name over and over.

4 **May 4–5, 2000: Two-and-a-Half Games**
Unlike regular-season games, playoff games that go to overtime don't end until someone scores. So fans at Game 4 of the 2000 Eastern Conference semifinals between the Philadelphia Flyers and Pittsburgh Penguins really got their money's worth. They were treated to 92 minutes of overtime hockey, meaning the teams played more than two full games. The Flyers finally won it on a goal by Keith Primeau — at 2:35 a.m.

5 **May 10, 1979: Too Many Men**
Less than three minutes from eliminating the three-time defending champion Canadiens in Game 7 of the semifinals, Boston was whistled for too many men on the ice. Montreal star Guy Lafleur then tied the game on the power play, and teammate Yvon Lambert won the series in OT.

6 **April 23, 1964: Down But Not Out**
With his Maple Leafs facing elimination in Game 6 of the Stanley Cup finals, Bobby Baun broke his ankle blocking a Red Wings shot. He returned to score the OT winner, as the Leafs forced Game 7 and went on to win their third straight Cup.

Top 10 Coaches

1 Scotty Bowman
St. Louis Blues (1967–71), Montreal Canadiens (1971–79), Buffalo Sabres (1979–87), Pittsburgh Penguins (1991–93), Detroit Red Wings (1993–2002)

Over a career that spanned five decades, Bowman set the bar for coaching excellence. And then he raised it higher and higher until he retired from the bench in 2002. He holds coaching records for most wins (1,244), playoff wins (223), and Stanley Cup titles (nine) — records that are unlikely to ever be broken. Coaching five different teams over his career, he was able to take four of them to the Stanley Cup finals. He won championships with the Canadiens, Penguins and Red Wings, making him the only professional coach in any sport to lead three different franchises to titles. A masterly strategist and motivator, Bowman has left a stamp on the game that will last a long time.

2 Toe Blake

Blake coached the Canadiens for 13 seasons, winning Stanley Cups in eight of them. Adding his three championships as a player, he had his name engraved on the Cup 11 times.

3 Al Arbour

On the New York Islanders' bench during their historic run of four consecutive Stanley Cups in the early 1980s, Arbour returned to the bench at age 75 for one game in 2007, becoming the oldest man to coach an NHL game.

4 Jack Adams

The only man to win Stanley Cups as a player, coach, and general manager, Adams coached the Red Wings to titles in 1936, '37, and '43. When the NHL introduced a coach of the year award in 1973–74, they named it after him.

5 Fred Shero

Nicknamed the Fog, the longtime Philadelphia Flyers coach — who led the team to two Stanley Cups — was a trailblazer. He was one of the first coaches to introduce film study and bring on a full-time assistant coach.

6 Punch Imlach

Imlach was so demanding of his players that one quit the NHL for four years because of the coach's harsh tactics. Still, it's impossible to ignore Imlach's success. He won four Cups in Toronto, including the Maple Leafs' last, in 1967.

7 Anatoli Tarasov

The Father of Russian Hockey, Tarasov laid the groundwork for the Soviet teams that dominated during the 1960s, '70s, and '80s. In 1974, he was inducted into the Hockey Hall of Fame.

8 Mike Babcock

Before Babcock became the second-fastest coach to reach 500 NHL wins in December 2014, he won a Cup with Detroit in 2008 and coached Team Canada to Olympic gold medals in 2010 and '14.

9 Dick Irvin

After 11 years coaching Chicago and Toronto, Irvin moved to Montreal in 1940 and helped turn around a team that had won just 10 games the year before. In 15 seasons with the Canadiens, Irvin won three Stanley Cups.

10 Glen Sather

Wayne Gretzky's first NHL coach, Sather helped guide the superstar and the Edmonton Oilers to four championships in the 1980s. He has been the general manager of the New York Rangers since 2000.

Top 10 Memorable Trades

1. Wayne Gretzky to Los Angeles, 1988
Fresh off his team's fourth Stanley Cup in five years, cash-strapped Edmonton Oilers owner Peter Pocklington shocked the hockey world when he pulled off a trade that would fundamentally change the NHL. Sending Gretzky to L.A. immediately lifted the Kings' profile and helped popularize hockey in America.

2. Eric Lindros to Philadelphia, 1992
The most hyped prospect since Mario Lemieux, the big, solid winger — nicknamed the Next One — entered the 1991 draft saying he didn't want to play for the Quebec Nordiques, who had the top pick. They selected him anyway, but when he refused to sign for a year, Quebec traded Lindros to the Flyers for six players, two picks, and $15 million.

3. Patrick Roy to Colorado, 1995
On Dec. 2, 1995, Montreal suffered its worst home defeat, losing 11–1 to Detroit. Roy let in five goals in the first period, but he wasn't pulled from the game until the score was 9–1 in the second period. Furious that the team left him in for so long, the Canadiens' goalie stormed off the ice. On his way out, he stopped by the team president and told him, "This is my last game in Montreal." The Canadiens traded the Hall of Famer to the Avalanche four days later.

4. Phil Esposito to Boston, 1967
The playmaking center became the centerpiece in arguably the most lopsided trade in NHL history. The Bruins received the 25-year-old Esposito (a Future Hall of Famer and five-time scoring champion), Ken Hodge (a onetime 50-goal scorer), and Fred Stanfield (a cluctch postseason performer) from the Chicago Blackhawks for three players.

5. Mark Messier to New York, 1991
After watching a sluggish 1991–92 season opener, Rangers general manager Neil Smith pulled the trigger on a long-negotiated trade to acquire the Oilers' captain and five-time Cup champion. Messier made an immediate impact in New York, leading the team to league's best record and winning the Hart Trophy as MVP in his first season.

6. Ralph Backstrom to Los Angeles, 1971
Sam Pollock, general manager of the Montreal Canadiens, sent productive defenseman Ralph Backstrom to the sinking Kings for next to nothing. Why? Backstrom had asked for a trade and Pollock owned the first-round pick of the woeful Oakland Seals in the forthcoming draft. He wanted the Kings to finish ahead of Oakland, so the Seals' pick would be the first overall. It worked, and Montreal scored Guy Lafleur.

7. Doug Gilmour to Toronto, 1992
The Calgary Flames winger had been in a long, bitter contract dispute with the team for months before he asked for a trade. Calgary struck a deal with the Maple Leafs that involved 10 players switching teams. It was the largest trade in NHL history.

8. Joe Thornton to San Jose, 2005
After signing Thornton to a three-year contract in August, the Bruins — who were in last place and desperate to shake things up — traded him three months later. Thornton was good in Boston and better with the Sharks. He finished the season with a league-high 125 points and became the only player to win the Hart Trophy playing with two teams in one season.

9. Jaromir Jagr to Washington, 2001
Growing tired of Pittsburgh, the Penguins' dynamic winger asked for a trade repeatedly during the 2000-01 season. He was granted his wish in July, when he was dealt to the Capitals.

10. Cam Neely to Boston, 1986
At the time, the trade was more about the Vancouver Canucks getting star center Barry Pederson. But in hindsight, Boston got a player who would be a franchise cornerstone for the next decade.

Top 10 Go

1 Patrick Roy
Known for his fiery competitiveness, the Hall of Fame goalie set the bar for clutch play. Over his 20-year career, Roy won four Stanley Cups, two each with the Montreal Canadiens and the Colorado Avalanche. His 151 playoff wins are unlikely to be matched for a long time. A three-time winner of the Vezina Trophy (awarded to the best goaltender in the league), he also won three Conn Smythe Trophies as the playoff MVP. That's more than even Wayne Gretzky. Roy's legacy also includes popularizing the butterfly style, in which a goalie drops to his knees to protect the bottom of the goal. After retiring, Roy became the coach of the Colorado Avalanche. In his first season he added another trophy to his case: the Jack Adams Award, which is handed out to the best coach in the league.

2 Jacques Plante
The Montreal netminder during the franchise's dynasty days, Plante led the Canadiens to six Cups from 1953 to '60. He was known as a great innovator, often venturing out of the crease to play the puck, instructing defensemen behind the play, and wearing a goalie mask regularly. In 1962 he became the first goalie to win both the Vezina Trophy and the Hart Trophy (given to the MVP) in the same season. His jersey number 1 was retired by the Canadiens in '95.

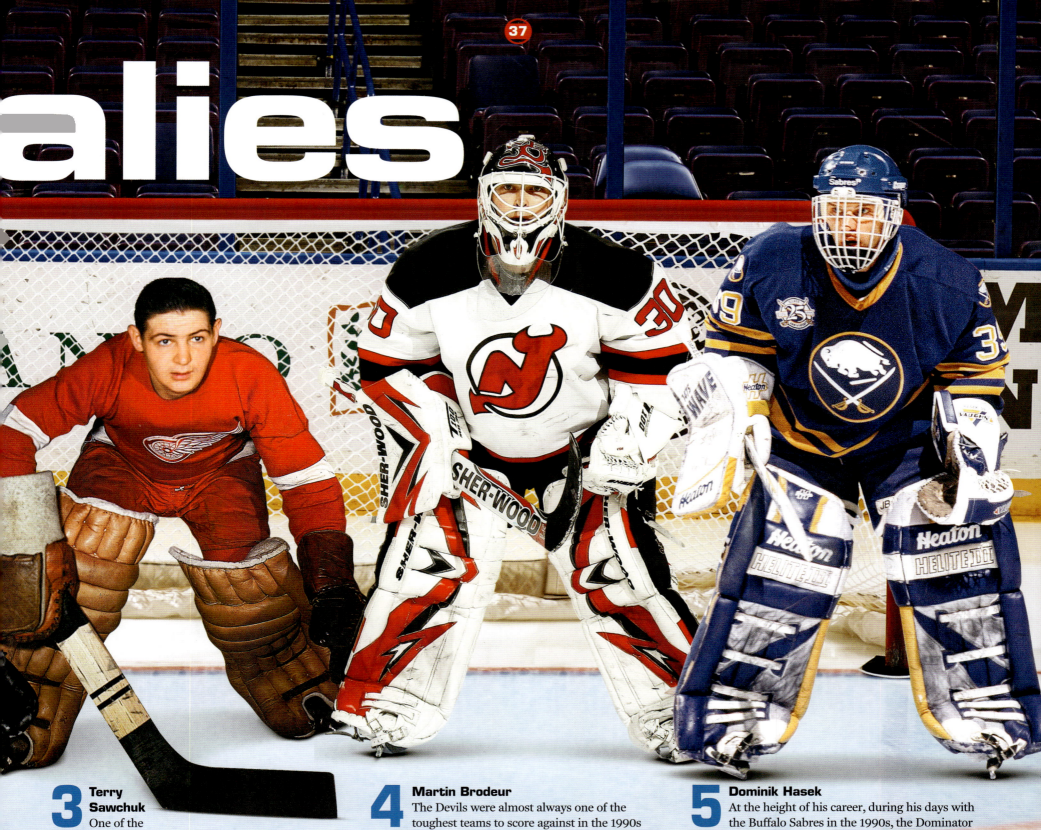

alies

3 Terry Sawchuk
One of the stingiest goaltenders in league history, the longtime Detroit Red Wing kept opponents off the scoreboard 115 times, including the playoffs. His most impressive feat came during the 1952 postseason, when Sawchuk led the Red Wings on a flawless 8–0 run, allowing just five goals and recording four shutouts in sweeps of the Toronto Maple Leafs and Canadiens.

4 Martin Brodeur
The Devils were almost always one of the toughest teams to score against in the 1990s and 2000s. Part of that was due to the team's defensive system, but a larger part was due to Brodeur. After a 22-year career, he retired in 2015 as the league's all-time leader in games (1,266), wins (691), and shutouts (125). His adeptness at handling the puck away from the net inspired the league to institute a rule curtailing the practice in 2005.

5 Dominik Hasek
At the height of his career, during his days with the Buffalo Sabres in the 1990s, the Dominator was untouchable. Although he had an unconventional style — diving, flailing, and even head-butting pucks to keep his net empty — it worked. In 1998, he became the first goalie to win back-to-back Hart Trophies, a feat that has never been matched. His career .922 save percentage remains a modern record for NHL goalies with at least 300 starts.

6 **Ken Dryden**
His career on the
ice was relatively short,
lasting just seven full seasons. But it
was memorably excellent: Dryden won
the Vezina Trophy five times. He
made quite a first impresssion,
winning the Conn Smythe Trophy
before winning the Calder Trophy
for rookie of the year. (Dryden came
up from the minors to lead the
Canadiens to the Stanley Cup in 1971,
then became their starter the following
fall.) He was later elected a member of
Canada's Parliament.

7 **Glenn Hall**
On November 7, 1962, Hall, then Chicago's
netminder, left the ice in the first period of a
game against Boston with a back injury. That ended
his incredible streak of 502 consecutive complete
games played. Nicknamed Mr. Goalie, Hall won the
Vezina Trophy three times and was part of three
Stanley Cup winners. He also earned a Conn Smythe
Trophy in '68, despite the fact that his Blues were
swept by the Canadiens in the Stanley Cup finals.

8 **Vladislav Tretiak**
The best goaltender never to play in the National Hockey League, Tretiak was the outstanding last line of defense for the famed Soviet Union national teams that won three Olympic gold medals and 10 world championships. He retired from the game in 1984, at age 32, five years before the U.S.S.R. allowed its players to join the NHL. In '89 he became the first non-NHL Russian player inducted into the Hall of Fame.

9 **Bernie Parent**
In the mid-1970s the Philadelphia Flyers goalie strung together two of the most impressive seasons in NHL history. Awarded the Vezina Trophy in '74 and '75, he also led Philadelphia to back-to-back Stanley Cups, earning Conn Smythe honors both seasons. He posted shutouts in both Cup-clinching games, and his dominance inspired a popular Philly bumper sticker that proclaimed, ONLY THE LORD SAVES MORE THAN BERNIE PARENT.

10 **Grant Fuhr**
The netminder for the Gretzky-era Oilers, Fuhr won five Stanley Cups in Edmonton. In his best season, 1987–88, he led the league with 40 wins and finished ahead of Gretzky in Hart Trophy voting. (Mario Lemieux won the top prize that year.) But he proved to be equally effective without the benefit of Edmonton's juggernaut offense. After signing with St. Louis in '95, he went on to play 79 games that season, a record that stands today.

Top 10 HAIR

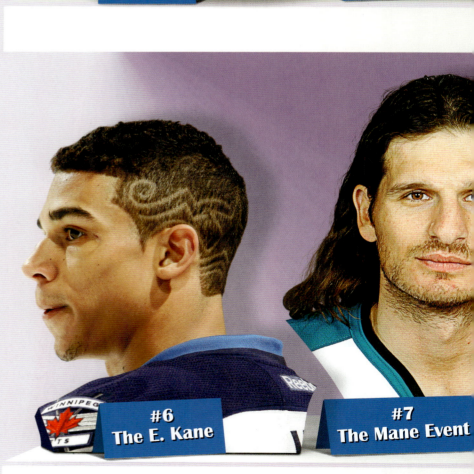

#1 The Jagr

#2 The Lafleur

#6 The E. Kane

#7 The Mane Event

1 Jaromir Jagr
The man. The myth. The mullet. During his dominant days of the 1990s, Jagr sported the all-time best coif, letting his curls grow out so long, they covered his name on the back of his jersey. Eventually, Jagr cleaned up his look for the latter part of his career.

2 Guy Lafleur
His long golden hair, wind-swept as he made his patented rushes up the ice, inspired his nickname, *le Démon Blond* (the Blond Demon). The look came to symbolize his supremacy in the league.

3 Mike Commodore
His messy, bushy, bright orange curls — with matching beard in the playoffs! — were so distinctive, they became the identifying feature of an otherwise unremarkable defenseman.

4 Barry Melrose
Still going strong after more than 20 years, Melrose's slicked back mullet — now with a touch of gray — may be the most enduring of hockey's iconic hairdos.

5 Maurice Richard
Perhaps this slick, aerodynamic hairdo helped the speedy Richard earn his nickname: Rocket.

6 Evander Kane
Kane introduced a fresh twist on "hockey hair," getting intricate designs such as stars and racing stripes shaved into the sides of his head.

7 Mike Ricci
In 2005, the longtime center had his hair cut so he would be believable as a 1950s hockey player in a movie about Maurice Richard. It was the first time he'd had his mane fully trimmed in 13 years. "I am not a big fan of haircuts," he explained. Gee, ya think?

8 Ron Duguay
One of the last NHL players to skate without a helmet, Duguay had a signature long, curly look.

9 Kerry Fraser
Thanks to his heavy use of hair spray, the longtime NHL referee once said proudly, "I could skate in a hurricane and [my hair] would never move."

10 Scott Hartnell
His mane inspired a Philadelphia Flyers' promotional giveaway in 2009 at a game against the Florida Panthers. The first 5,000 fans received a Scott Hartnell wig. The game was a sellout.

#3
The Commodore Fro

#4
The Melrose

#5
The Rocket

#8
The Duguay

#9
The Fraser

#10
The Hartnell

Top 10 Non-NHL GAMES

1

The Miracle on Ice
1980 Olympic medal round
U.S.A. vs. U.S.S.R.

On February 22, 1980, in Lake Placid, New York, a group of American amateur college players pulled off one of the most stunning upsets in the history of sports. The Soviet Union had won five of the seven previous Olympic gold medals. And two weeks before the 1980 Games, the team crushed the U.S. 10–3 in an exhibition. But on that special evening in the medal round of the Olympics, the U.S. knocked off the Soviets 4–3. They did it by scoring two unanswered goals in the third period and riding the goaltending of Jim Craig. He made 36 saves, including nine in the final period. Two days later the U.S. again fought back from a deficit to beat Finland, earning America's first gold medal in hockey since 1960. The team and the game were so memorable that in 2004 their story was made into a movie, *Miracle*.

2 1972 Summit Series, Game 8

Canada vs. U.S.S.R.

The Summit Series was the first true best versus best international series. Over the course of eight games, the national team of the Soviet Union took on Canada's NHL stars. The Soviets sent a message by handily winning the first game 7–3. After the first five games, in fact, the U.S.S.R. held a 3-1-1 lead. But Canada fought back to tie the series, setting up a winner-take-all Game 8. In front of a hostile Soviet crowd, Canada trailed by two goals going into the third period. But goals from Phil Esposito and Yvan Cournoyer erased the deficit. As the clock ticked down, Canadian winger Paul Henderson smacked in a rebound to win the game with just 34 seconds left. The goal remains one of the most famous in hockey history.

6 2014 Olympic women's final

Canada vs. U.S.A.

Team USA was in search of its first gold medal since the inaugural women's Olympic tournament in 1998. Canada had won three golds in a row. The U.S. held a two-goal lead late in the third period, when Canada staged a frantic comeback. Brianne Jenner cut the lead in half with 3:26 left. Then after Kelli Stack of the U.S. missed an empty-net opportunity by a matter of inches, Canadian winger Marie-Philip Poulin scored the equalizer. Eight minutes into overtime, she scored again on a 5-on-3 power play to deny the U.S. once more.

7 2009 IIHF World Junior Championship semifinal

Canada vs. Russia

With less than three minutes left in a back-and-forth third period, Russia scored a go-ahead goal that would have sealed the game — if not for Canada's Jordan Eberle. The winger tied the game with just 5.4 seconds left, then scored the shootout winner.

3 2010 Olympic final
Canada vs. U.S.A.

When U.S. winger Zach Parise sent the game into overtime by scoring with just 24.4 seconds left in regulation, the gold medal matchup in Vancouver went from good to great. And when Canada's Sidney Crosby shot the puck through U.S. goalie Ryan Miller's pads at 7:40 of the extra frame, the game became an instant classic. In front of a boisterous home crowd, Team Canada won the nation's 14th gold medal of the 2010 Games, topping the previous mark for most golds won by a country at a Winter Games. (The old record of 13 had been set by the Soviet Union in 1976, and Norway tied it in 2002.)

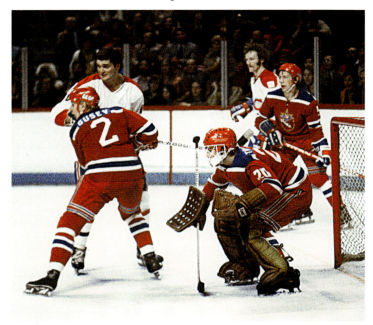

4 Super Series '76
CSKA Moscow vs. Montreal Canadiens

On New Year's Eve, the top team in the Soviet Union visited the team that would go on to win the Stanley Cup. The result is the best game ever to end in a tie. CSKA weaved and passed while Montreal pressed and shot. And although the Canadiens outshot the Red Army 38–13, they could not get a winner past goalie Vladislav Tretiak. When the final horn sounded, the score was 3–3.

5 1987 Canada Cup finals, Game 3
Canada vs. U.S.S.R.

The six-nation tournament culminated in a three-game series between the imposing Soviet Union team and the star-studded Canadian squad, which was led by Wayne Gretzky and Mario Lemieux. Skating on the same line, the two talents were responsible for almost a third of Canada's goals during the series, including three from Lemieux in Game 2. But their most memorable connection came late in Game 3. With the score tied 5–5 and less than 90 seconds left in regulation, Gretzky dropped a sweet pass to Lemieux, who netted the series winner.

8 1996 World Cup finals, Game 3
U.S.A. vs. Canada

In the rubber match of the best-of-three finals, the U.S. scored four unanswered goals in the last four minutes to come from behind and beat Canada 5–2. Led by sniper Brett Hull, who scored the tying goal, and goalie Mike Richter, the tournament MVP, the 1996 World Cup title was the greatest achievement for USA Hockey since the 1980 Miracle on Ice.

9 2010 IIHF World Junior Championship final
U.S.A. vs. Canada

A year after his heroics against Russia, Team Canada's Jordan Eberle struck again. He scored two goals in the last three minutes of regulation to tie the game 5–5. Unlike in the 2009 semis, however, Canada wouldn't come out on top. Team USA defenseman John Carlson broke in with Derek Stepan on a 2-on-1 and snapped home the game-winner at 4:21 into overtime. The goal gave the U.S. its second World Junior championship.

10 2009 NCAA Frozen Four final
Boston University vs. Miami (Ohio) University

Miami had a comfortable 3–1 lead with a minute left in regulation. But in just 42 stunning seconds, the Terriers scored twice to tie the game, and BU's Colby Cohen won the Terriers the title with an OT goal.

Top 10 Nicknames

THE GREAT ONE

1 Wayne Gretzky

When he was just 10 years old, he earned the nickname from a small-town reporter. It stuck — through his junior career, his one year in the World Hockey Association and 20 NHL seasons. At every stop the Great One lived up to his billing. In one season as a peewee player, he scored a whopping 378 goals. As an NHL player, Gretzky continued to rewrite record books, holding more than 60 NHL marks when he retired in 1999. His nickname became so iconic that for years, incoming phenoms — such as Eric Lindros and Sidney Crosby — had been dubbed the Next One. Although Gretzky had other nicknames during his career (Mr. Wayne-derful and the White Tornado, because of the white gloves he wore as a peewee), none had the lasting power of the Great One.

THE FINNISH FLASH

5 Teemu Selanne

In 1992–93, the 22-year-old winger from Helsinki, Finland, scorched through the NHL. He scored a rookie-record 76 goals for the Winnipeg Jets. He scored 608 more in 21 NHL seasons, finally retiring with the Anaheim Ducks in 2014. Always quick to shoot, score, and smile for the camera, the Finnish Flash was electrifying to watch.

BOOM BOOM

6 Bernie Geoffrion

When Geoffrion was a junior player, a local sportswriter took to calling him Boom Boom, describing the noise his slap shots made: one *boom* when the stick struck the puck; another *boom* when the puck hit the boards. Geoffrion used the shot — which he claimed he invented — to his advantage throughout his career. He twice led the league in goals and appeared in 11 All-Star Games.

The Golden Jet

7 Bobby Hull

Given Hull's wavy blond hair, dazzling speed, and howitzer shot, the Golden Jet was a natural nickname for the Blackhawks winger. It became even more appropriate in 1972. After 15 years in the NHL — during which he became the first player to score more than 50 goals in a season — Hull jumped to the Winnipeg Jets of the rival WHA.

Mr. Hockey

2 **Gordie Howe**
Playing in the NHL until he was 52 years old, the Detroit Red Wings legend lived and breathed hockey for most of his life. He was so well-known by his nickname that he once received a fan letter that was simply addressed to: Mr. Hockey, Detroit, Mich. His wife, Colleen, had his nickname trademarked years later. And she registered Mrs. Hockey for herself.

THE ROCKET

3 **Maurice Richard**
Ray Getliffe played 393 games for the Boston Bruins and the Montreal Canadiens in the 1930s and '40s, but he's best remembered for inspiring one of hockey's most enduring nicknames. Watching his Canadiens teammate take off with the puck, Getliffe likened Richard to a rocket. A reporter overheard him, and before long, all of Montreal knew its star simply as the Rocket.

The Chicoutimi Cucumber

4 **Georges Vezina**
Born in Chicoutimi, Quebec, in 1887, the Canadiens goalie was known for his calm demeanor — he was cool as a cucumber. Leading the NHL with a 3.93 GAA in the league's inaugural season in 1917–18, Vezina eventually became the namesake of the trophy awarded to the top goaltender every year. He was part of the first class inducted into the Hockey Hall of Fame, in 1945.

The Golden Brett

8 **Brett Hull**
Hull had a slap shot that reminded people of his father, Bobby. And what better name for the son of the Golden Jet than Golden Brett? The son, however, never liked the nickname. In his 2003 autobiography, he explained: "Dad is the Golden Jet and he is the greatest left wing ever to play. It's just not cool for me to use a derivative of his nickname." That didn't stop others from using it, though.

Grapes

9 **Don Cherry**
No one is sure if it's a play on his last name or if it is short for Sour Grapes, but Cherry has had the nickname since his days as a minor league defenseman. It has endured throughout his career as a coach and broadcaster. For years he hosted a weekly TV show in Canada called *Don Cherry's Grapevine*, and he still has a radio show called *Don Cherry's Grapeline*.

THE DOMINATOR

10 **Dominik Hasek**
The Dominator was a play on Hasek's first name, but it was also an appropriate way to describe his game. The only goalie to win back-to-back Hart Trophies as the league's MVP, Hasek was an intimidating force in net for the Buffalo Sabres. In 735 career games he had a .922 save percentage, best among netminders with at least 300 games played.

TOP 10 FAMILIES

1

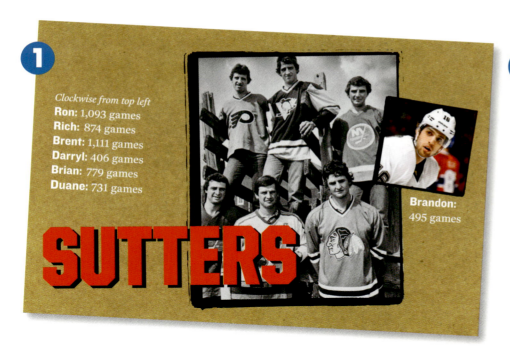

Clockwise from top left
Ron: 1,093 games
Rich: 874 games
Brent: 1,111 games
Darryl: 406 games
Brian: 779 games
Duane: 731 games

Brandon: 495 games

SUTTERS

2

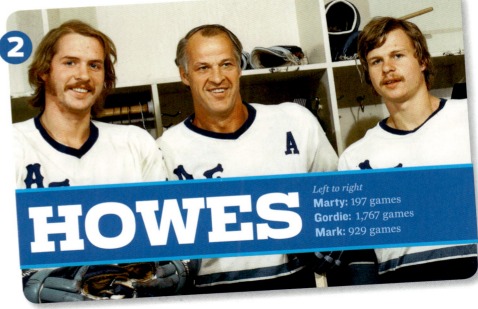

HOWES

Left to right
Marty: 197 games
Gordie: 1,767 games
Mark: 929 games

5

Left to right
Jordan: 607 games
Jared: 2 games
Eric: 846 games
Marc: 540 games

STAALS

7

APPS

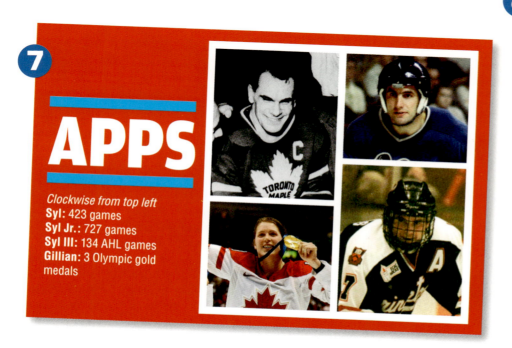

Clockwise from top left
Syl: 423 games
Syl Jr.: 727 games
Syl III: 134 AHL games
Gillian: 3 Olympic gold medals

8

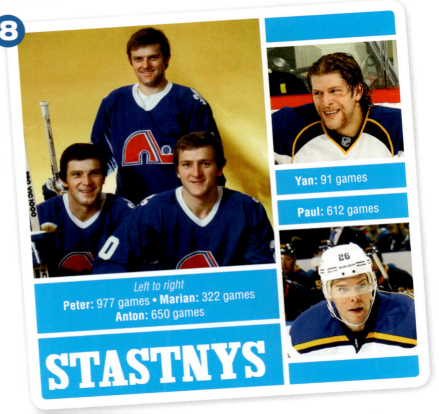

Yan: 91 games

Paul: 612 games

Left to right
Peter: 977 games • **Marian:** 322 games
Anton: 650 games

STASTNYS

3 HULLS

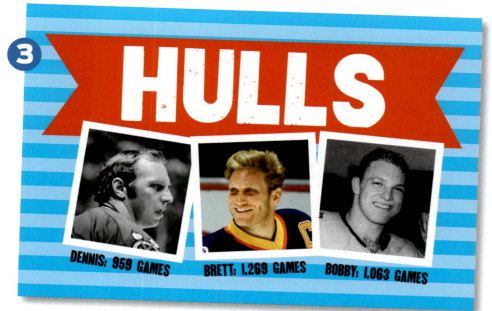

DENNIS: 959 GAMES **BRETT:** 1,269 GAMES **BOBBY:** 1,063 GAMES

4 Richards

Henri: 1,256 games • Maurice: 978 games

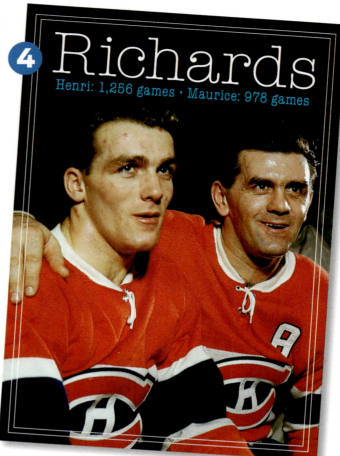

6 Espositos

Phil: 1,282 games **Tony:** 886 games

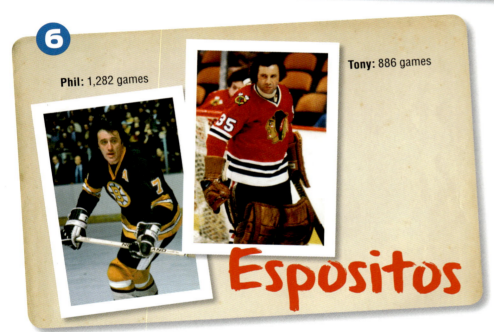

9 Geoffrions

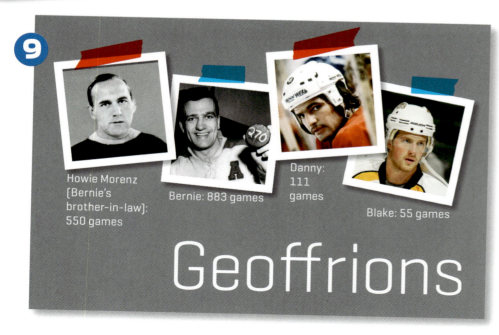

Howie Morenz (Bernie's brother-in-law): 550 games

Bernie: 883 games

Danny: 111 games

Blake: 55 games

10 Granatos

Tony: 773 games

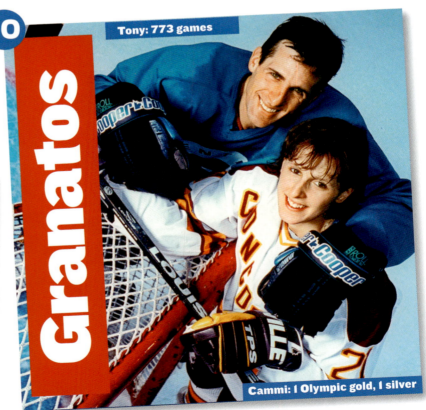

Cammi: 1 Olympic gold, 1 silver

Top 10 Captains

1 Mark Messier
Edmonton Oilers (1988–91)
New York Rangers (1991–97, 2000–04)
Vancouver Canucks (1997–2000)

Messier played for three teams in his 25-year career, and he wore the C on his jersey for each of them. The Hall of Famer remains the only player to captain two franchises to Stanley Cup victories. He first captained the Oilers to the championship in 1990 and then helped end the Rangers' 54-year Cup drought in '94. It was during that postseason that Messier forged his legend as hockey's greatest leader. With New York facing elimination in Game 6 of the Eastern Conference finals, Messier famously guaranteed a win against the Devils. After 40 minutes the Rangers trailed 2–1. That was when Messier went out and delivered on his promise, scoring a third-period hat trick to force Game 7, which New York won in double overtime. Then, when faced with another Game 7 in the Stanley Cup finals against Vancouver, Messier scored the Cup-clinching goal. The image of an elated Messier accepting the Cup on the ice became one of the most iconic in hockey history. And he has been considered the league's consummate leader ever since. In 2006 the NHL introduced the Mark Messier Leadership Award.

2 Steve Yzerman
Detroit Red Wings (1986–2006)

In 1986, when he was just 21 years old, Yzerman became the youngest full-time captain in NHL history. He held the position in Detroit for 19 years, leading the Red Wings to Stanley Cups in 1997, '98, and 2002. Known for always putting the needs of the team above his own, Yzerman was more than just an offensive whiz who had six straight 100-point seasons. He was one of the best two-way centers in the game, contributing even after his scoring fell off later in his career. When he retired in 2006, he did so as the longest-tenured captain in NHL history.

4 **Bobby Clarke**
Philadelphia Flyers (1972–79, 1982–84)
Clarke captained Philadelphia's famed Broad Street Bullies, who won back-to-back Stanley Cups in 1974 and '75. Embodying the Flyers' mix of skill and toughness, Clarke had 1,210 points (still a franchise record), served 1,453 penalty minutes, and won three Hart Trophies during his 15-year career. After retiring, Clarke moved to the Flyers' front office, where he is now the team's senior vice president. He remains a franchise hero even now, more than 30 years after his final game.

3 **Jean Beliveau** *Montreal Canadiens (1961–71)*
Montreal's gentle giant, Beliveau was voted captain by his teammates in 1961. The move paid off: The Canadiens won five Stanley Cups in the next 10 seasons. Beliveau had a reputation as a great scorer (he was the second player to record 1,000 points), but he was even better known for being a respectful leader and hockey's classiest ambassador. For more than 50 years, Beliveau answered each piece of fan mail he received.

8 **Joe Sakic**
Quebec Nordiques and Colorado Avalanche (1992–2009)
A hallmark of a great NHL captain is selflessness. And few others could challenge Ordinary Joe in that category. When the Avalanche won the Stanley Cup in 2001, Sakic — as the team captain — was entitled to the first lap with the trophy. But instead of skating with the Cup, he immediately handed it to Ray Bourque, who had played 22 years without winning a Cup. Sakic, who is still the franchise leader in games, goals, and points, also captained the Avs to the 1996 championship.

7 **Wayne Gretzky** *Edmonton Oilers (1983–88); Los Angeles Kings (1989–96)*
Gretzky only learned what it took to win a Stanley Cup when he caught a glimpse of a champions' locker room. After being swept by the Islanders in the 1983 finals, Gretzky didn't see celebration in New York's dressing room. He saw a roomful of battered and bruised players with ice bags. Understanding their sacrifices helped him lead the Oilers to four championships in five years. When he moved to Los Angeles, he captained the team for seven years — and led a hockey revolution in the United States.

5 Mario Lemieux *Pittsburgh Penguins (1988–94, 1995–97, 2001–06)*
Lemieux built a legendary résumé over his 17 seasons with the Penguins: six scoring titles, three Hart Trophies, two Conn Smythe Trophies and two Stanley Cups. But what made his accomplishments even more impressive was that he did it all while beating cancer in 1993 and while suffering from often debilitating back pain for most of his career. The example he set as a survivor inspired not only his teammates but also all hockey fans.

6 Denis Potvin *New York Islanders (1979–87)*
On a team with plenty of starpower, the physical defenseman stood out. Potvin captained the Islanders to four-straight Stanley Cups in the early 1980s. New York never missed a postseason while Potvin wore the C on his sweater. And when they got to the playoffs, the Islanders meant business: They won a record 19 straight playoff series from 1980 to '84. A three-time Norris Trophy winner as the league's top defenseman, Potvin was the first blueliner to amass 1,000 career points. He was inducted into the Hockey Hall of Fame in 1991.

9 Nicklas Lidstrom *Detroit Red Wings (2006–12)*
When Steve Yzerman retired, he left big skates to fill for Detroit's next captain. But if anyone could do the job, it was the defenseman the Red Wings nicknamed Mr. Perfect. A seven-time Norris Trophy winner, Lidstrom rarely made mistakes on the ice. He was always respected throughout the league, and in 2008, the Swede became the first European-born player to captain a Stanley Cup champion.

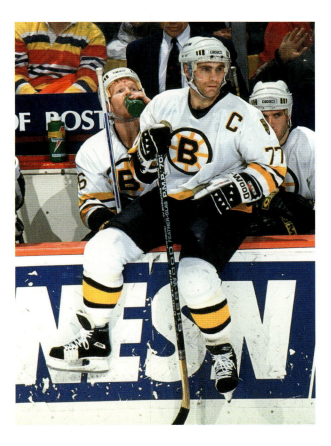

10 Ray Bourque *Boston Bruins (1985–2000)*
During Bourque's 15-year tenure as the Bruins' captain, the team made the postseason every year but one. Boston advanced to the Stanley Cup finals twice, but both times the Bruins lost to Edmonton. Bourque finally won a Stanley Cup with Colorado in 2001, when he was 40 years old. Though the winning team captain traditionally gets the first lap with the Cup, Avalanche captain Joe Sakic gave the trophy to Bourque, a respectful nod to a leader who deserved a captain's turn with the Cup.

TOP 10
DON CHERRY

For more than 30 years, Don Cherry has been a Saturday night staple for millions of Canadian hockey fans. He appears on "Coach's Corner," a segment shown during the first intermission of *Hockey Night in Canada*. His on-air comments are often colorful — and so is his wardrobe. The 81-year-old former coach of the Boston Bruins is known for his vibrant suits and jackets, which he has custom-made from material he personally selects at a tailor shop called The Coop Ink in Toronto. His collection of outfits has grown to fill all but one of the closets and an entire spare bedroom in his home.

1

2

3

4

5

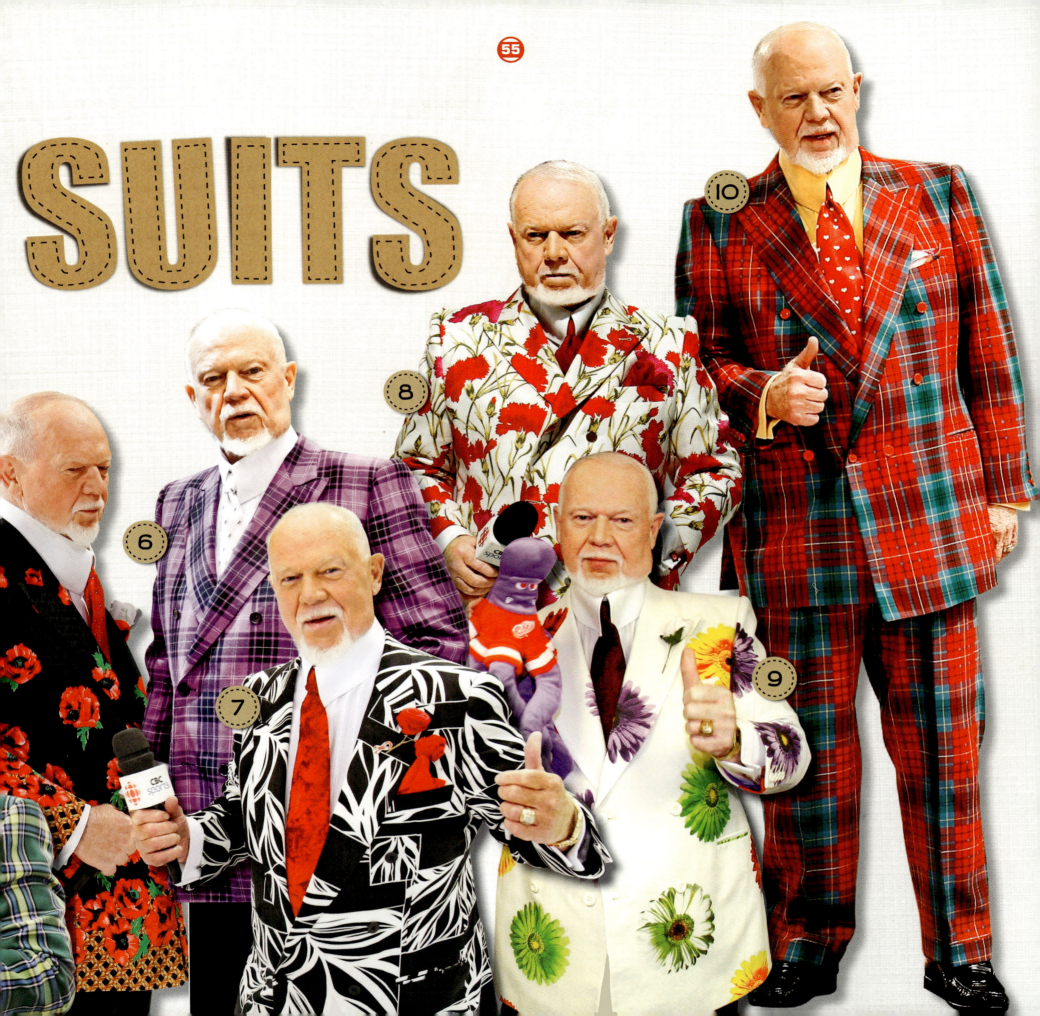

SUITS

TOP 10 LINES

1

Ted Lindsay • Sid Abel • Gordie Howe
Detroit Red Wings

In a city known for automotive plants, Detroit's Production Line churned out goals for the dominant Red Wings in the late 1940s and early '50s. Abel, in his 30s and nearing the end of his career, centered two talented young wingers who played with grace and toughness. In '49–50 the trio finished the season one-two-three in the league in scoring, combining for 92 goals. That spring they led Detroit to its fourth Stanley Cup. For the next two seasons Howe, Abel, and Lindsay were again the Red Wings' top scorers, and they won another Stanley Cup in '52. The group was split up when Abel was traded to Chicago that off-season to become player-coach of the Blackhawks. Later on, the three legends were reunited in the Hockey Hall of Fame.

THE PUNCH LINE

2

Toe Blake • Elmer Lach • Maurice Richard
Montreal Canadiens

In the mid-1940s the Canadiens' famed Punch Line was no laughing matter for opponents. In 1944–45 Blake, Lach, and Richard were the top three scorers in the NHL, with Lach leading the way with 80 points. But his feat was overshadowed by Richard, who became a legend by scoring 50 goals in 50 games.

THE LILCO LINE

3 **Clarke Gillies • Bryan Trottier • Mike Bossy**
New York Islanders
The arrival of Bossy, a first-round draft choice in 1977, completed the Islanders' top line. Named for a Long Island power company, the line was lights out, leading New York to four straight Stanley Cups in the early '80s.

THE DYNASTY LINE

4 **Steve Shutt • Jacques Lemaire • Guy Lafleur**
Montreal Canadiens
Winning four Cups in the late 1970s, the Canadiens were carried by their high-scoring top line. Lafleur dazzled with six straight 100-point seasons, and Shutt was a sublime finisher, scoring 60 goals in '76–77. But it was veteran center Lemaire who anchored the unit with his brainy play.

THE FRENCH CONNECTION

7 **Rick Martin • Gilbert Perreault • Rene Robert**
Buffalo Sabres
In 1974–75, the Sabres' trio scored 131 goals and then combined for 128 the following season. But as fearsome a line as it was, the three never seemed to connect in the playoffs, making it to the finals just once during their reign.

THE KRAUT LINE

8 **Woody Dumart • Milt Schmidt • Bobby Bauer**
Boston Bruins
Put together on a line when they were in the minors, the three young players were inseparable. They shared everything from ice time to a one-room apartment near Boston. In 1939–40, the trio became the first linemates to finish one-two-three in scoring. Schmidt led the way with 52 points.

THE KLM LINE

5 Vladimir Krutov •
Igor Larionov •
Sergei Makarov
Soviet Union
The internationally known —
and feared — top line of
the Soviet Union's Red
Army team played with
grace. When the three
swooped and swerved
around the ice, they
made hockey look like
ballet.

THE TRIPLE CROWN LINE

6 Charlie Simmer • Marcel Dionne • Dave Taylor
Los Angeles Kings
When the 24-year-old left wing Simmer joined All-Star Dionne and
high-scoring winger Taylor on the Kings' top line in January 1979, the three
clicked instantly. Simmer, who had scored 25 points in four previous seasons,
finished the season with 48 points in 38 games.

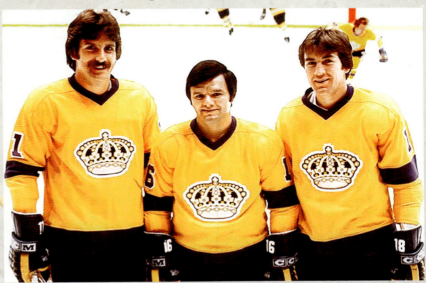

WAYNE'S LINE

9 Esa Tikkanen • Wayne Gretzky • Jari Kurri
Edmonton Oilers
Gretzky and Kurri were the dynamic duo of the Oilers' dynasty. They combined
for 300 points four times in the 1980s. They played with several linemates — and made
them all look good — but it was Tikkanen, a Finnish left wing, who rode with them to two
of Edmonton's four Stanley Cup titles.

THE ESPO LINE

10 Wayne Cashman • Phil Esposito • Ken Hodge
Boston Bruins
From the late 1960s through the mid-'70s, the Bruins were
led by the game's top defenseman, Bobby Orr. But Boston also relied on
a trio that was anchored by Hall of Fame center Esposito, who topped
the NHL in scoring five times.

TOP 10 PLAYERS WHO HAVE NEVER WON A CUP

1 Marcel Dionne

Detroit Red Wings, Los Angeles Kings, New York Rangers (1971–89)

He was drafted second behind Guy Lafleur in 1971. And while Lafleur won five Stanley Cups with the Montreal Canadiens, Dionne never made it past the second round of the playoffs. He scored 731 goals, had 1,771 points, and won a scoring title in 1979–80. But hidden away on bad teams, Dionne never made an impact in the playoffs. In nine postseason runs, all but one with L.A., Dionne averaged less than a point per game, a far cry from his regular-season average of 1.31.

2 Peter Stastny

Quebec Nordiques, New Jersey Devils, St. Louis Blues (1980–95)

In 15 seasons, Stastny never made it to the Stanley Cup finals, despite being the most prolific scorer of the 1980s not named Gretzky. In the postseason, he scored 105 points in 93 games, ranking 12th all-time in career playoff points per game.

3 Adam Oates

Detroit Red Wings, St. Louis Blues, Boston Bruins, Washington Capitals, Philadelphia Flyers, Anaheim Ducks, Edmonton Oilers (1985–2004)

Oates played in 1,337 games, scored 1,420 points, and made playoff appearances for six teams. It took him 13 seasons to make it to the Stanley Cup finals (with Washington in 1998), but the Capitals were swept. Five years later he lost in the finals again, with Anaheim.

4 Dale Hawerchuk
Winnipeg Jets, Buffalo Sabres, St. Louis Blues, Philadelphia Flyers (1981–97)

The No. 1 overall pick in 1981 spent nine years in Winnipeg, taking the Jets to the playoffs eight times. But playing in the same division as Wayne Gretzky's Oilers made things difficult. From 1981 to '90, the Jets met Edmonton six times in the playoffs and lost each time. In that span, Winnipeg won just four of 26 playoff games against the Oilers.

5 Mark Howe
Hartford Whalers, Philadelphia Flyers, Detroit Red Wings (1979–95)
His father, Gordie, won four Stanley Cups, but Mark, a Hall of Famer who played 16 seasons, never won one. But he did get close. In 1987, Howe's Flyers fought back from a 3–1 series deficit to force a do-or-die Game 7. Philadelphia actually struck first in that game, scoring early in the first period, but it wasn't long before the Oilers came back to win, 3–1.

6 Mike Gartner
Washington Capitals, Minnesota North Stars, New York Rangers, Toronto Maple Leafs, Phoenix Coyotes (1979–98)

In 19 seasons Gartner never made it to the Stanley Cup finals, but he played a part in a championship. In 1994, as a Ranger, he was dealt to Toronto so the Rangers could acquire winger Glenn Anderson. He then had to watch as the Rangers captured the Cup without him.

7 Daniel Alfredsson
Ottawa Senators, Detroit Red Wings (1995–2014)
The right wing spent all but one of his 18 seasons in Ottawa, where he set franchise records in goals and assists. Alfredsson led the Senators to the 2007 Cup finals, but they lost to Anaheim. Alfredsson signed with Detroit for one last shot, but the Red Wings lost in the first round.

8 Mats Sundin
Quebec Nordiques, Toronto Maple Leafs, Vancouver Canucks (1990–2009)

In 13 seasons with Toronto, Sundin set the Maple Leafs' franchise record for points, with 987. But the eight-time NHL All-Star failed to take Toronto past the conference finals.

9 Brad Park
New York Rangers, Boston Bruins, Detroit Red Wings (1968–85)
The defenseman won a Memorial Cup as a junior player in 1967 and was elected to the Hall of Fame in 1988. But in 17 NHL seasons Park never played for a Stanley Cup champion.

10 Curtis Joseph
St. Louis Blues, Edmonton Oilers, Toronto Maple Leafs, Detroit Red Wings, Phoenix Coyotes, Calgary Flames (1989–2009)

Cujo's .917 postseason save percentage ranks 13th all-time among goalies with at least 50 games. Though he won 63 playoff games, he never appeared in the finals.

Top 10 Shootout Artists

1 T.J. Oshie
Right wing (2008–present)

The St. Louis Blues star earned a spot on the U.S. Olympic team in 2014, in no small part because of his skill in the shootout. Oshie finds the back of the net on more than half of his one-on-one attempts (52.5% of them, to be exact). Taking Oshie to the Olympics in Sochi, Russia, paid off big time for the U.S. In a round-robin game against Russia, Oshie scored on four of his six attempts. In international play, unlike in the NHL, shooters can be reused after the initial three players make their attempts. So after the teams were tied through the first round, Team USA coach Dan Bylsma opted to send Oshie out for every shot. The winger finally won it for the U.S. in the eighth round, beating Russian goalie Sergei Bobrovsky and handing the home team a crushing defeat.

2 Jonathan Toews
Center (2007–present)

Toews is 40 for 80 in NHL shootouts in his career, just another facet of the Chicago Blackhawks star's incredibly well-rounded game. He has never scored fewer than 23 goals in a season, wins 56.9% of his face-offs, and has even won the Selke Trophy as the league's best defensive forward. His crowning one-on-one moment, however, came before he ever played an NHL game. In the 2007 World Junior semifinals, Toews scored three shootout goals in one game to help lift Canada over the United States.

3 Frans Nielsen
Center (2006–present)

The longtime New York Islanders sniper, who is 38 for 72 in shootouts in his career, doesn't rely on dipsy-doos and fancy dangles. He usually takes the simple forehand-to-backhand route, but he is so quick that he freezes the goalie in his tracks. He then seamlessly lifts his shot past the netminder — often leaving the goalie off-balance and flailing as he watches the puck go into the net behind him.

4 Pavel Datsyuk
Center (2001–present)

The Detroit Red Wings star possesses a bag full of tricks in the shootout, whether it's a slick heel-drag, a deke, a dangle, or the fake-out floater that he famously used against Chicago Blackhawks goalie Antti Niemi in 2010. It's no wonder that Datsyuk was successful in half of his shootout attempts in his first seven seasons. Though his pace has cooled, in his prime Datsyuk was the king of the shootout.

5 Zach Parise
Left wing (2005–present)

Only two players have been sent to center ice for a shootout more often than Parise, who has 90 attempts in his 10 seasons in the league. And it's easy to see why: Parise has converted 43.3% of his tries. That rate has helped cement his reputation as one of the league's most clutch performers. Parise has 49 career game-winning goals, including 15 scored in the late-season months of March and April.

6 Jussi Jokinen
Left wing (2005–present)

The Finnish winger arrived in the NHL the same season as the shootout rule: 2005–06. As a rookie with the Dallas Stars, Jokinen wowed the league by going 10 for 13 in shootouts. He's slowed down a bit, but he can still dazzle in a one-on-one battle. In December 2014, Jokinen tucked in a beautiful one-handed goal against the Washington Capitals in what became the longest shootout in NHL history (20 rounds).

7 Brad Boyes
Right wing (2003–present)

Since debuting with the San Jose Sharks, Boyes has bounced around the league, appearing with six teams in 11 years. But he has been a valuable shootout weapon at every stop. He has a success rate of 44.8%. Though he has averaged less than 17 minutes per game and has a negative plus-minus in his career, Boyes shines after overtime. With a pair of soft hands, he has uncanny control over the puck in open ice.

8 Radim Vrbata
Right wing (2001–present)

The 2009–10 Phoenix Coyotes were a tight checking team with a limited offense, which meant they were bound to take part in plenty of shootouts. Twenty of them, to be exact, which set a single-season record. And in 18 of those shootouts, the Coyotes dispatched Vrbata, who scored eight times. Over his career the winger, who made his first All-Star game in 2015, at the age of 33, has scored on 42.7% of his shootout attempts.

9 Erik Christensen
Center (2005–12)

Christensen was traded three times and waived once in his seven-season career, proving that specialists will always be in demand. (He suited up for the Pittsburgh Penguins, Atlanta Thrashers, Anaheim Ducks, New York Rangers, and Minnesota Wild.) Though he played fewer than 400 games, he still had 55 shootout attempts — and made 29 of them, for a stellar 52.7% success rate.

10 Patrick Kane
Right wing (2007–present)

His career shootout rate of 41.4% may not be extraordinary, but many of Kane's successful attempts are certainly memorable. Whether he is getting goalies to bite with a fake forehand or mesmerizing them with fancy stickwork as he closes in, the Chicago Blackhawks star relishes the opportunity to show off his incredible skill when every eye in the arena is set squarely on him.

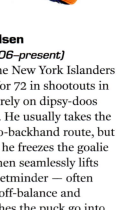

Gerry Cheevers
Boston Bruins

The goalie mask, which grew in popularity during the 1960s, was originally used solely for protection. That changed when Cheevers left a practice after taking a puck to the mask. When his coach insisted he return to the ice, Cheevers had trainer John Forristall draw stitch marks where the puck would have hit his face. It turned into a running gag. For every shot that ricocheted off his mask, Cheevers and Forristall drew a new set of stitches. Ever since, goalies have used their masks to make fashion statements.

2 Gilles Gratton
New York Rangers

Playing just 47 games from 1975 to '77, Gratton had a career goals-against average of 4.02. Far more impressive than his play was his inventive mask. It was inspired by a photo of a tiger he saw in *National Geographic*. The mask is credited with triggering a generation of masks that incorporated fierce animal faces.

Top 10
Goalie

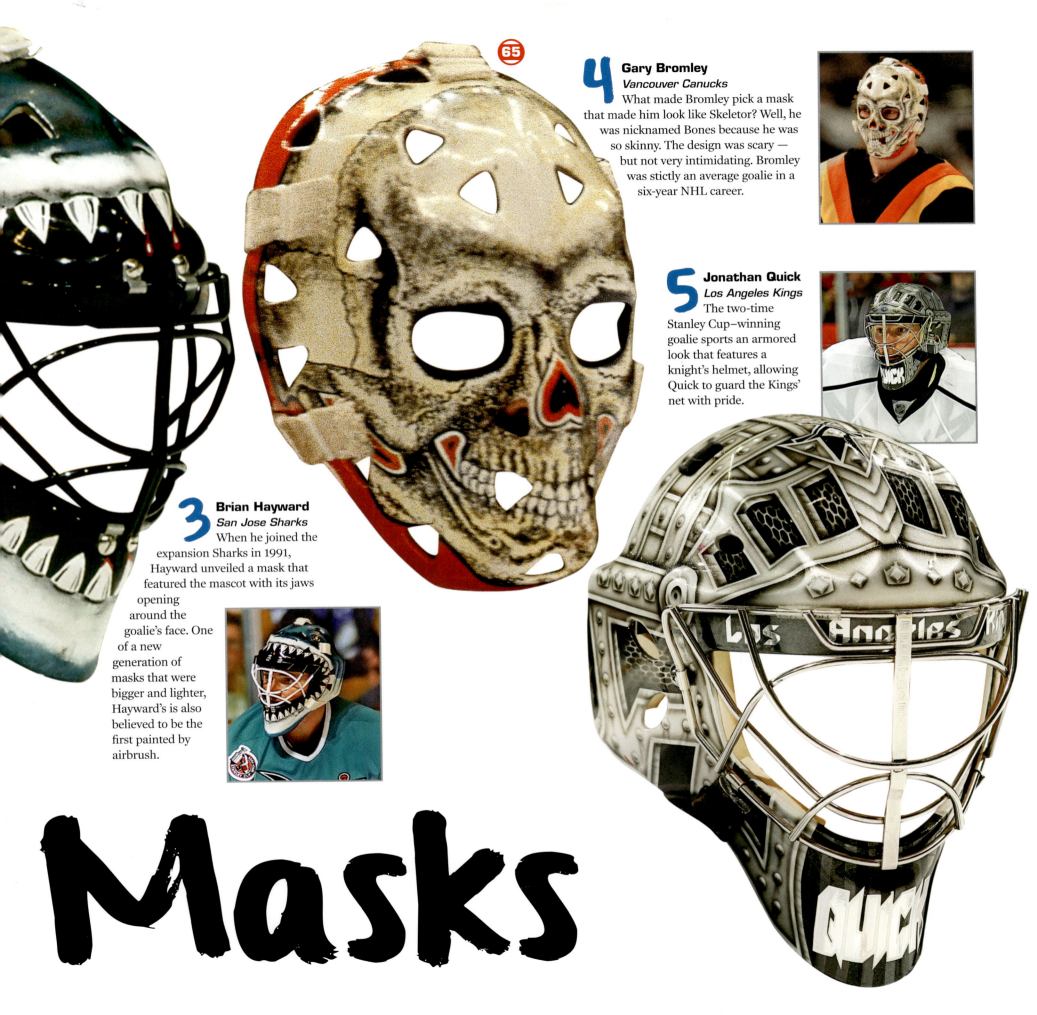

4 **Gary Bromley**
Vancouver Canucks
What made Bromley pick a mask that made him look like Skeletor? Well, he was nicknamed Bones because he was so skinny. The design was scary — but not very intimidating. Bromley was stictly an average goalie in a six-year NHL career.

5 **Jonathan Quick**
Los Angeles Kings
The two-time Stanley Cup–winning goalie sports an armored look that features a knight's helmet, allowing Quick to guard the Kings' net with pride.

3 **Brian Hayward**
San Jose Sharks
When he joined the expansion Sharks in 1991, Hayward unveiled a mask that featured the mascot with its jaws opening around the goalie's face. One of a new generation of masks that were bigger and lighter, Hayward's is also believed to be the first painted by airbrush.

Masks

Top 10 GOALIE MASKS

7 **Ryan Miller**
Team USA
At the 2010 Olympics in Vancouver, Miller went with a very patriotic design. Hidden in all of the red, white, and blue was a green clover. That was for Jim Craig, the Boston-area native who had a shamrock on his mask when he was the goalie for the 1980 U.S. Olympic champs.

6 **Andy Moog**
Boston Bruins
After seven successful seasons in Edmonton during the 1980s, Moog was traded to the Bruins in '88. Looking for a new helmet in Boston, he commissioned one from a local mask maker, Dom Malerba, who suggested painting a snarling bear face on the mask. The trend caught on in Boston, where several goalies have used the bear motif since.

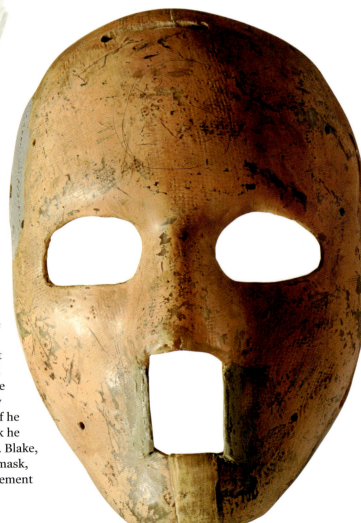

9 Mike Richter
New York Rangers

Playing in the Big Apple, Richter had no shortage of local icons to choose from when designing his mask. The Hall of Famer ultimately chose the Statue of Liberty. Simple yet sophisticated, the logo even inspired the Rangers to use a similar Lady Liberty logo on their alternate jerseys from 1996 through 2007.

8 Jonas Hiller
Anaheim Ducks

In November 2011, the Ducks' goalie wore a mask that featured photographs of his teammates — with mustaches drawn on their faces. It was part of Anaheim's Movember campaign, during which players grew mustaches in November to bring awareness to men's health issues. Since he joined the league in 2007, Hiller, who now plays for the Calgary Flames, has had some of the sleekest designs in the NHL, including a matte black mask with a gold cage.

10 Jacques Plante
Montreal Canadiens

Though goalies had occasionally worn protective masks in practice, Plante became the first to wear one regularly, in 1959. Facing the Rangers at Madison Square Garden in an early-season game, Plante took a shot to the face early in the first period. He then told Canadiens coach Toe Blake he would only return to the game if he could wear the mask he donned in practices. Blake, who didn't like the mask, relented, and a movement was born.

24

Top 10 Playoff Game

1 **1994 Eastern Conference finals**
The New York Rangers struck first, when defenseman Brian Leetch scored midway through the second period. But New Jersey Devils winger Valeri Zelepukin batted in a rebound to tie the game in the final seconds of regulation. It was the second time in the series that the Devils scored with an extra attacker in the final minute. But unlike in Game 1, which New Jersey won in double OT, the Rangers came out on top, as Stephane Matteau played the hero with a goal in the second overtime period.

7s

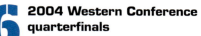

6 | 2004 Western Conference quarterfinals

With their backs against the wall, the Vancouver Canucks staved off elimination with a triple-overtime victory over the Calgary Flames in Game 6. In the thrilling deciding game, Vancouver winger Matt Cooke scored twice, including a goal with six seconds left to send the game to overtime. Despite the Canucks' late-game heroics, Calgary's Martin Gelinas won the series just 85 seconds into the extra frame.

7 | 1950 Stanley Cup finals

New York's Don Raleigh scored two overtime winners in the final series against Detroit. But he couldn't produce magic a third time in Game 7. In that game, the Red Wings' Pete Babando scored the Cup-winning goal in double overtime.

2 | 2013 Eastern Conference quarterfinals

In their first trip to the postseason in nine years, the Toronto Maple Leafs forced a Game 7 with the Boston Bruins. Before a hostile Boston crowd, the Leafs had a 4–1 lead early in the third period. The tide turned, however, after Bruins winger Nathan Horton scored with 10:42 left. With Boston's offense buzzing and Toronto on its heels, the Bruins threw 17 shots on goal in the period and scored two goals in the last 90 seconds of regulation. Boston won in overtime.

8 | 1987 Patrick Division semifinals

When the horn blew to signal the end of regulation of the matchup between the New York Islanders and the Washington Capitals, the game wasn't even halfway over. Finally, in the fourth overtime, Islanders star Pat LaFontaine blasted a slap shot past Washington goalie Bob Mason to win the marathon.

3 | 2010 Eastern Conference semifinals

The Bruins won the first three games of the series but watched their comfortable lead crumble away as the Philadelphia Flyers roared back and evened the series. In the deciding game, Boston took a three-goal lead, but the Flyers came back to win 4–3, becoming just the third team to win a playoff series after dropping the first three games.

4 | 1942 Stanley Cup finals

Long before Philadelphia's epic comeback in 2010, there were the 1942 Leafs, who dug themselves out of a three-game hole against the Detroit Red Wings in the finals. In Game 7, down a goal in the third period, Toronto scored three times to win the franchise's second Stanley Cup.

9 | 2002 Western Conference semifinals

The see-saw battle between the San Jose Sharks and the Colorado Avalanche was a showdown between two of the top goaltenders in the NHL. Colorado's Patrick Roy was nearing the end of his dominant career, while San Jose's Evgeni Nabokov was surging onto the scene. Roy won the duel, making 27 saves in a 1–0 shutout.

5 | 2009 Stanley Cup finals

It was déjà vu, as the Pittsburgh Penguins and the Red Wings met in the finals for the second straight year. But unlike in '08, when Detroit earned the ultimate prize, the Penguins held on during a furious third period in which they had just one shot on goal. The 2–1 win gave Pittsburgh its first Stanley Cup in 17 years.

10 | 2014 Western Conference finals

When Alec Martinez of the Los Angeles Kings scored the overtime winner against the Chicago Blackhawks, it was L.A.'s third Game 7 road win of the postseason. The Kings only needed five games to win their next series — and the Stanley Cup.

Top 10 TERRIBLE

1 Anaheim Mighty Ducks (1995–96) It's no surprise that a franchise named after a Disney comedy would have such funny, cartoonish uniforms. The third jerseys, with a duck bursting through the ice, were just plain awful.

2 New York Islanders (1995–97) When the team rebranded and unveiled a new logo, fans noticed that the stick-wielding fisherman bore an uncanny resemblence to the mascot of Gorton's fish sticks. That earned the Islanders the nickname Fish Sticks for years after.

6 Phoenix Coyotes (1998–2003) The team's abstract hockey-playing Coyote logo was bad enough. But Phoenix's third jerseys, which were green with trim that was supposed to evoke the desert, were even worse.

7 Edmonton Oilers (2001–07) Nothing says "Oilers" quite like what appears to be a giant gear streaking through outer space. With a teardrop on it. Well, maybe the tear drop was appropriate: Edmonton lost the Stanley Cup finals in 2006, the next-to-last season these third jerseys were worn.

3 Montreal Canadiens (2009)
These prison-striped jerseys were an homage to the 1912–13 Canadiens. Montreal wore them once in 2009. That was more than enough.

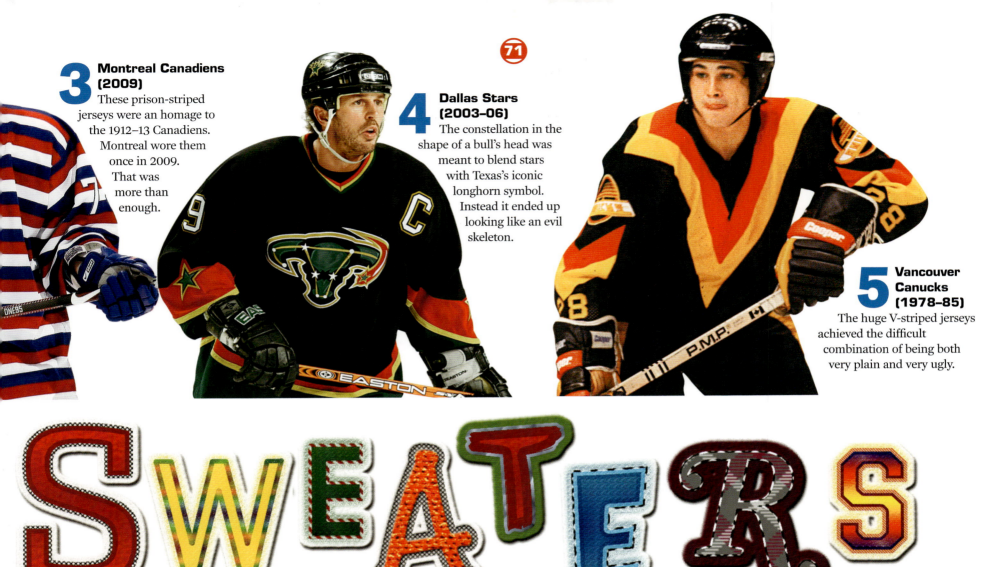

4 Dallas Stars (2003–06)
The constellation in the shape of a bull's head was meant to blend stars with Texas's iconic longhorn symbol. Instead it ended up looking like an evil skeleton.

5 Vancouver Canucks (1978–85)
The huge V-striped jerseys achieved the difficult combination of being both very plain and very ugly.

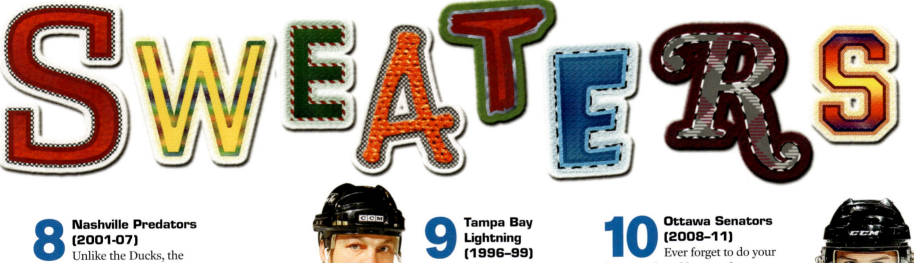

SWEATERS

8 Nashville Predators (2001-07)
Unlike the Ducks, the Predators are not run by Disney. But their saber-toothed tiger logo still looks as if it came from a cartoon. Even worse, though, is the color: a dull yellow the same hue as Dijon mustard.

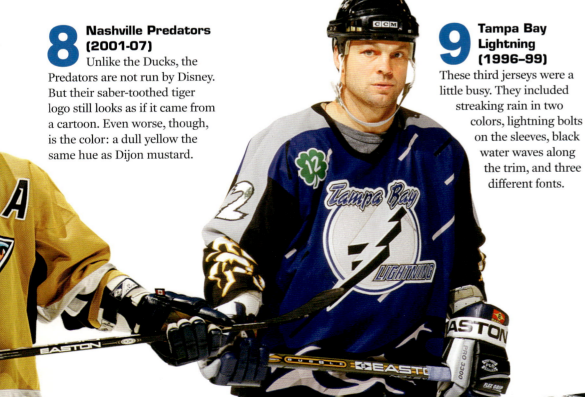

9 Tampa Bay Lightning (1996–99)
These third jerseys were a little busy. They included streaking rain in two colors, lightning bolts on the sleeves, black water waves along the trim, and three different fonts.

10 Ottawa Senators (2008–11)
Ever forget to do your homework and have to throw something down real quick when it's time to turn in your work? Looks like that happened here. And is *Sens* even a word?

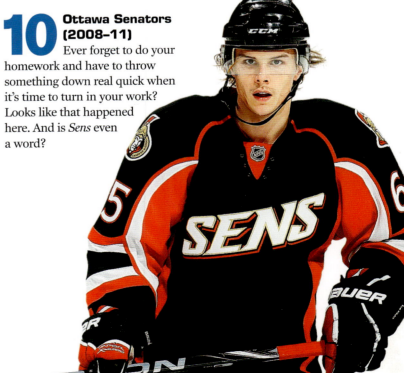

TOP 10
DOMIN
TEAMS

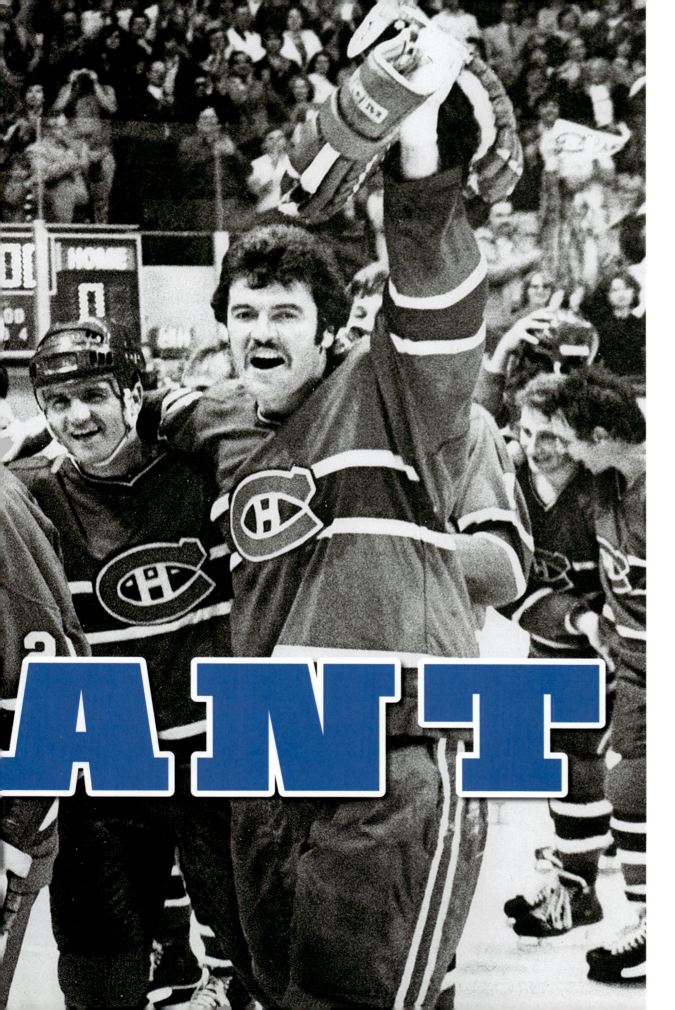

1

1976–77 Montreal Canadiens

With nine future Hall of Famers on the roster, and another in legendary coach Scotty Bowman, the 1976–77 Canadiens seemed to face their toughest competition in scrimmages at practice. Setting the NHL record for most team points, these Canadiens outscored opponents by 2.76 goals per game. In 94 games, including the playoffs, Montreal lost just 10 times, going 60-8-12 in the regular season and sweeping both the Blues and the Bruins in the postseason. In a three-month period from January to April '77, Montreal lost just one of 39 games. Led by the fearsome top line of Guy Lafleur, Steve Shutt, and Jacques Lemaire, the Canadiens were as hard-working as they were talented. Their victory over Boston in the Stanley Cup finals game them their second of four straight championships.

CLUB DE HOCKEY CANADIEN 1976-77
F. JACQUES COURTOIS PRES. SAM POLLOCK V.P. & G.M.
JEAN BELIVEAU V.P. & D.C.R. SCOTTY BOWMAN COACH
PETER BRONFMAN DIR. EDWARD BRONFMAN DIR.
CLAUDE RUEL D.P. FLOYD CURRY A.G.M. RON CARON A.
YVAN COURNOYER LARRY ROBINSON GUY LAFLEUR
PIERRE BOUCHARD REJEAN HOULE YVON LAMBERT
ROBERT GAINY JACQUES LEMAIRE GUY LAPOINTE
KENNETH DRYDEN RICK CHARTRAW WILLIAM NYROP
MICHEL LAROCQUE PIERRE MONDOU SERGE SAVARD
STEPHEN SHUTT MARIO TREMBLAY MURRY WILSON
DOUGLAS JARVIS MICHAEL POLICH JIM ROBERTS
PETER MAHOVLICH PIERRE MEILLEUR ASST. TRA.
DOUGLAS RISEBROUGH EDWARD PALCHAK H. TRA.

2 1983–84 Edmonton Oilers

The Oilers came close to raising the Stanley Cup after the 1982–83 season, cruising into the finals with only one playoff loss. But they proceeded to be swept by the New York Islanders, who held the Oilers to just six goals in the four games. The following season Edmonton got revenge, taking the finals from the Islanders in five games — and ending New York's run of four straight titles. The Oilers were the most explosive offensive team the league had ever seen. They scored an NHL-record 446 goals and boasted the first trio of teammates to score at least 50 goals: Wayne Gretzky (92), Glenn Anderson (54), and Jari Kurri (52). Aside from a bad February road trip, on which Edmonton dropped five straight games, the Oilers lost back-to-back games just one time that season. In the playoffs, Gretzky, who had been held without a goal by the Islanders in '83, found redemption. He scored four times in the finals and had 35 points in 19 postseason games.

3 1977–78 Montreal Canadiens

The year after their historic season, the Canadiens proved that 1976–77 was no fluke. Montreal followed up its 60-win campaign with 59 victories in '77–78 and finished with just three fewer points. And the outcome in the postseason was again the same. The Canadiens made quick work of the Detroit Red Wings and Toronto Maple Leafs before facing the Bruins in the finals. This time, Boston managed to squeeze out two wins in front of their fans. But the mighty Canadiens won the clincher, 4–1, at Boston Garden.

7 1955–56 Montreal Canadiens

No team had more influential players than this group. Featuring legendary Hall of Famers Jacques Plante, Jean Beliveau, Bernie Geoffrion, and Maurice Richard, the Canadiens won the first of their five consecutive Stanley Cups.

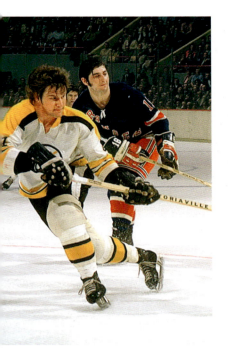

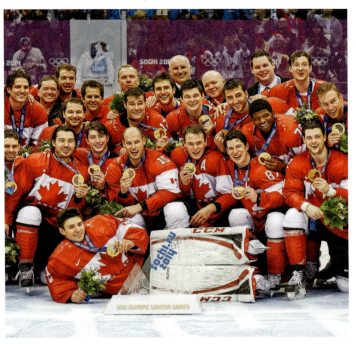

4 **1971–72 Boston Bruins**
The Bruins, led by defenseman Bobby Orr, went 54-13-11 in the regular season and dropped just three games in the playoffs, winning their second Cup in three years.

5 **2014 Canadian Olympic team**
The defending gold medalists entered the tournament in Sochi, Russia, with high expectations. And Team Canada delivered. Outscoring its six opponents 17-3, Canada sealed its second straight gold medal with a 3–0 win over Sweden. Carey Price led goalies in the Olympic Games with a .972 save percentage, and defenseman Drew Doughty scored a team-high four goals.

6 **1981–82 New York Islanders**
In the prime of the Islanders' dynasty days, the team seemed unbeatable. It didn't matter if they were playing a physical game or a finesse game — New York could win either way. In the season in which they won the third of their four straight Stanley Cups, the Isles lost just 16 games. Led by Mike Bossy and Bryan Trottier, who combined for 114 goals, New York had the second-best goal differential in the league.

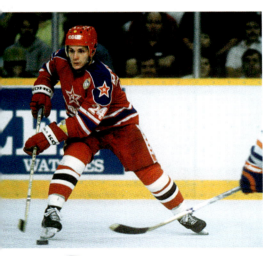

8 **1985–86 CSKA Moscow**
In 1986 the Soviet juggernaut went to Canada to take on the NHL's best in the Super Series. The Soviets went 5–1, with wins over the defending Stanley Cup champion Edmonton Oilers and the eventual Cup champs, the Montreal Canadiens.

9 **1951–52 Detroit Red Wings**
The Wings, who won 44 of 70 games during the regular season, became the first team to put together a flawless 8–0 run in the playoffs. Goaltender Terry Sawchuk was superb. He gave up five goals and had four shutouts in Detroit's two sweeps.

10 **1974–75 Philadelphia Flyers**
The team that had bullied its way to a Stanley Cup the previous year proved it could win by playing clean, fundamental hockey too. Behind the excellent goaltending of Bernie Parent, who had four shutouts in the postseason and won his second straight Conn Smythe Trophy as playoff MVP, the Flyers muzzled Buffalo's French Connection line (center Gilbert Perreault and wings Richard Martin and Rene Robert) in the finals. Though they have made six trips to the finals since, Philadelphia has yet to win Cup number three.

Top 10 Cup Day Stories

1
Kick the Cup
1905 Ottawa Silver Seven

Even before the NHL was established in 1917, Lord Stanley's Cup was the ultimate prize in hockey for teams across Canada. One of the earliest dynasties, the Ottawa Silver Seven, won the trophy four times in a row, beginning in 1903. Perhaps all of that success made the players take the Cup for granted. While celebrating their third championship, one of them wondered if he could kick the silver bowl across Ottawa's Rideau Canal. When he drop-kicked the trophy, it landed on the frozen canal. It wasn't until the next morning that they went back and retrieved it, beginning a long history of memorable stories involving the Stanley Cup.

2
A Holy Grail
1996 Colorado Avalanche

In 1995 the NHL formalized the tradition of giving each member of the championship team 24 hours with the Stanley Cup. The following year Avalanche defenseman Sylvain Lefebvre, who had contributed five assists in the postseason, used the opportunity to take the Cup to church. In his hometown in Quebec, Lefebvre arranged to have it act as the holy font in the baptism of his infant daughter, Alexzandra.

3
The Cup Doesn't Float
1992 Pittsburgh Penguins

Days after the Penguins won their second straight Stanley Cup, captain Mario Lemieux threw a celebratory pool party. Before long, winger Phil Bourque took the trophy up to the top of the pool's 25-foot waterfall and lifted it above his head. At the urging of his teammates, he tossed the Cup into the water and watched it sink quickly into the deep end. It took five or six players to fish out the Cup, and the silver tarnished because of the chlorine. But it was nothing a little polish couldn't fix.

4
Lord Stanley's Flower Pot
1907 Montreal Wanderers

The Cup-winning Wanderers brought the trophy to the home of a photographer after reclaiming the title from the Kenora Thistles. But after having their portraits taken, the players forgot to take the Cup when they left. For months it remained at the photographer's home, where his mother turned it into a beautiful flower pot.

5
Russian Road Trip
1997 Detroit Red Wings

The strict regime of the Soviet Union kept the stars of the famed Red Army teams from playing in the NHL until 1989. But by 1997 more than 60 Soviet-born players were skating in the league. So when Detroit won the Cup in '97 with a handful of Russian stars on its roster, three of them — center Igor Larionov, winger Slava Kozlov, and defenseman Slava Fetisov — took the Stanley Cup home with them to Russia. In its first trip to Moscow, the trophy was greeted by thousands of fans and visited historic sites such as Red Square.

6
A Curse is Born
1940 New York Rangers

The Rangers played their first season in 1926–27 and won the Stanley Cup three times in the next 13 years. But their championship in 1940 would be the start of a historically long drought. Legend has it, the owners of Madison Square Garden were so thrilled to have finally paid off a $3 million mortgage to the building that they celebrated by burning the mortgage in the Stanley Cup. Seen as dishonoring the trophy, it began the Curse of the Rangers. New York would not win another championship for 54 years.

7
No Horseplay
1994 New York Rangers

Just as soon as the Rangers' curse was broken, New York winger Ed Olczyk invited another Cup controversy. A horse enthusiast, he brought the 35-pound trophy to Belmont Park, where he posed for a picture with the 1994 Kentucky Derby winner, Go For Gin. In the photo the horse had his mouth buried in the bowl, appearing to eat. Olczyk, however, insisted that no horse used the Cup as a feeding dish.

8
Diapers Required
1964 Toronto Maple Leafs

After taking a photo with his baby son sitting in the trophy's bowl, eight-time champion Red Kelly saw that his son had an accident in the Cup. And in 2008, Red Wings forward Kris Draper said his newborn daughter did the same while not wearing a diaper. But don't worry. In 2010 a Chicago newspaper conducted a germ test on the Cup and found it to be surprisingly clean.

9
Roadside Attraction
1924 Montreal Canadiens

Today, the Stanley Cup is always accompanied by an official handler from the Hockey Hall of Fame, who makes sure the trophy is never lost or forgotten. In 1924 the Canadiens could have used someone like that. After winning the Cup in the Ottawa Auditorium, the team promptly left for Montreal to celebrate. The team car carrying the Cup, however, got a flat tire on the way. As players worked to fix it, they took the trophy out and sat it roadside. It wasn't until they arrived in Montreal that they realized they left without their prize. Luckily, the Cup was still by the side of the road when they rushed back.

10
Inside And Out
1992 Pittsburgh Penguins

Phil Bourque, the instigator of the Cup's pool-party episode, had another memorable moment during that championship summer. During his turn with the trophy, he noticed a rattling noise coming from inside, so he investigated. He removed the pedestal and stuck his head into the deep base of the trophy with a pen light in his mouth. Seeing a nut had become loose, he fixed the issue. But Bourque also noticed the names of those who repaired the trophy engraved on the inside. He picked up a screwdriver and carved in his own message: "Enjoy it . . . Phil 'Bubba' Bourque, '91 Penguins." He figured that would make him the only person with his name on both the outside and inside of the Stanley Cup.

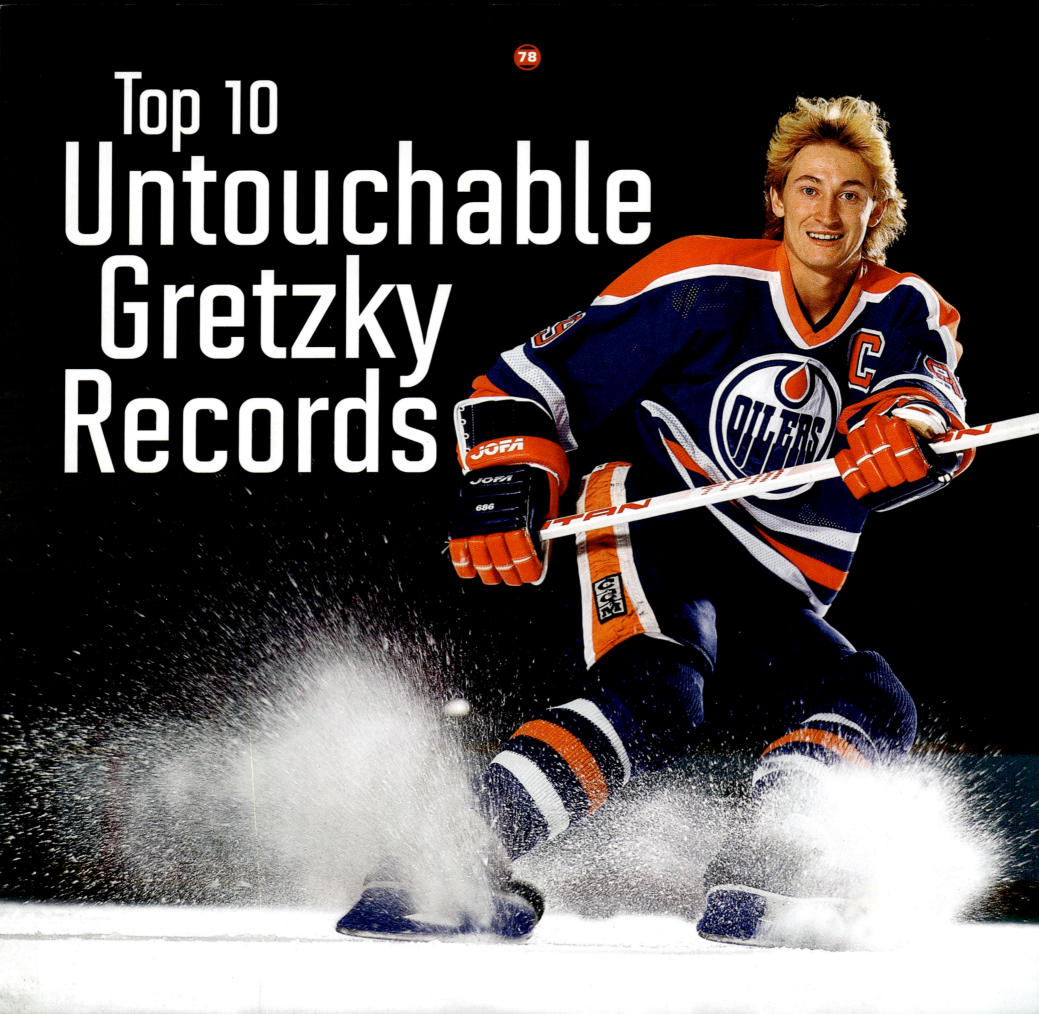

Top 10
Untouchable
Gretzky
Records

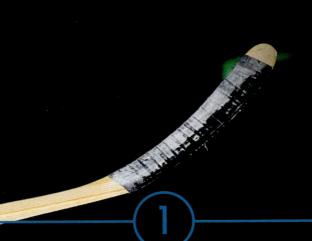

1

Most Career Points
2,857

In 20 seasons, Wayne Gretzky wrote and rewrote the NHL record book, becoming the most decorated scorer in league history. When he retired in 1999, Gretzky held 61 NHL records — many of which will likely never be broken. Gretzky's most impressive figure, and the least likely to fall, is his career total of 2,857 points. (He amassed it with the Edmonton Oilers, Los Angeles Kings, St. Louis Blues, and New York Rangers.) At the time of his retirement, Gretzky had 1,007 more points than Gordie Howe, the previous all-time leading scorer. And in the 16 years since, no NHL player has come within 970 points of Gretzky's mark. With 1,802 points, Jaromir Jagr is the only active player who is even in Gretzky's orbit — and he's still more than 1,000 points behind. To break Gretzky's record, a player would have to average about 115 points per year for 25 seasons. Since 2000, only four players have scored more than 115 in a single season.

2

Most consecutive seasons with 40 or more goals
12

From 1979–80 to 1990–91, a stretch that included four Stanley Cups and nine scoring titles, Gretzky didn't see a down year. He scored 718 goals during that span.

3

Longest consecutive point-scoring streak
51 GAMES

Mario Lemieux went 46 straight games with a point in 1989–90, but no one else has ever come within 20 games of Gretzky's record.

4

Most career playoff points
382

Though he ranks 16th in postseason games played, Gretzky has 87 more playoff points than any other NHL star.

5

Most career goals, including playoffs
1,016

As skilled as he was at passing (he had twice as many assists as goals), no one came close to matching the Great One's ability to find the net.

6

Most points in one season, including playoffs
255

Only two players have scored more than 200 points in a season: Lemieux (218 in 1988–89) and Gretzky, who did it six times.

7

Most Art Ross Trophies
10

Gretzky won the Art Ross Trophy as the top scorer in exactly half the seasons he played. The previous record, held by Gordie Howe, was six. Only four active NHL players — Sidney Crosby, Jaromir Jagr, Evgeni Malkin, and Martin St. Louis — have won multiple Art Ross Trophies. Jagr took home five, while the others have each won twice.

8

Most single-season goals, including playoffs
100

Since Gretzky set the benchmark in 1983–84, the year he won his first Stanley Cup, Brett Hull and Lemieux have fallen just short, scoring 97 in '90–91 and '88–89, respectively.

9

Most assists in one season
163

In 1985–86, Gretzky had so many assists, he would have won the scoring title even if he had not scored a single goal. Only Lemieux and defenseman Bobby Orr have ever picked up more than 100 assists in a season. The only player in recent years to approach that milestone was Joe Thornton, who had 96 assists in 2005–06.

10

Most three-or-more goal playoff games
10

While Gretzky holds the record, he also played a significant role in second place. Jari Kurri, Gretzky's longtime linemate, is tied with Canadiens legend Maurice Richard for second place on the playoff hat trick list, with seven.

Photo Credits

Cover: Andy Marlin/NHLI/Getty Images (face-off)
Back Cover: Dave Reginek/NHLI/Getty Images (rivalries); Bruce Bennett Studios/Getty Images (goalie masks); Damian Strohmeyer for Sports Illustrated (hardest shots); Manny Millan for Sports Illustrated (greatest players); David E. Klutho for Sports Illustrated (Cup Day stories)
Title Page: David E. Klutho for Sports Illustrated
Copyright page: Jonathan Daniel/Getty Images
Table of Contents: Dilip Vishwanat/Getty Images
Greatest: Manny Millan for Sports Illustrated (Gretzky); Tony Triolo for Sports Illustrated (Orr); Bettmann/Corbis (Howe); David E. Klutho for Sports Illustrated (Lemieux); AP (Richard, Hull); Bruce Bennett Studios/Getty Images (Beliveau, Harvey); Denis Brodeur/NHLI/Getty Images (Lafleur); Tim DeFrisco for Sports Illustrated (Roy)
Traditions: Jim Davis/The Boston Globe/Getty Images (handshake line); David E. Klutho for Sports Illustrated (octopus, Winter Classic); Jonathan Daniel/Getty Images (national anthem); Lou Capozzola for Sports Illustrated (playoff beards); Jamie Sabau/NHLI/Getty Images (hat trick hats); Harry How/Getty Images (Cup to captain); Jeff Vinnick/NHLI/Getty Images (Stanley Cup day); Bill Smith/NHLI/Getty Images (don't touch trophies); Andre Ringuette/Getty Images (Kate Smith)
Single-Game Performances: Barry Gray/Sun Media Corporation (Sittler); Gregory Shamus/NHLI/Getty Images (Crosby); Robert Beck for Sports Illustrated (Oshie); Philadelphia Flyers Archives (Hill); Andy Devlin/NHLI/Getty Images (Gagner)
Rivalries: Jared Wickerham/Getty Images (Bruins–Canadiens); David E. Klutho for Sports Illustrated (Red Wings–Blackhawks, Red Wings–Avalanche, USA–Canada, women); Denis Brodeur/NHLI/Getty Images (Canadiens–Maple Leafs, Canadiens–Nordiques); Andy Devlin/NHLI/Getty Images (Oilers–Flames); Justin K. Aller/Getty Images (Flyers–Penguins); Scott Levy/NHLI/Getty Images (Rangers–Islanders); Melchior DiGiacomo/Getty Images (U.S.S.R.–Canada)
Smiles: John D. Hanlon for Sports Illustrated (Clarke); Gregg Forwerck/NHLI/Getty Images (Ovechkin, Couturier); AP (Hull, Howe); Scott Cunningham/NHLI/Getty Images (Carcillo); Bill Wippert/Buffalo Sabres/AP (Barnaby); Al Bello/Getty Images (Daneyko); Bruce Bennett/Getty Images (Keith); Bruce Bennett Studios/Getty Images (Ricci)
Fastest Skaters: Scott Cunningham/NHLI/Getty Images (Bure); Elsa/NHLI/Getty Images (Fedorov); Glenn Cratty/Getty Images (Gartner); Robert Beck for Sports Illustrated (Hagelin); Steve Babineau/NHLI/Getty Images (Cournoyer); Bruce Bennett/Getty Images (Grabner); Tony Triolo for Sports Illustrated (Orr); Francis Miller/The Life Picture Collection/Getty Images (Hull); David E. Klutho for Sports Illustrated (MacKinnon); AP (Morenz); Joseph Gareri/Getty Images (background)
Little Guys: Len Redkoles/NHLI/Getty Images (St. Louis); Lane Stewart for Sports Illustrated (Richard); Steve Babineau/NHLI/Getty Images (Fleury); Melchior DiGiacomo/Getty Images (Cournoyer); B. Bennett/Getty Images (Dionne); AP (Lindsay); Imperial Oil–Turofsky/Hockey Hall of Fame (Worters); Pictorial Parade/Getty Images (Worsley); Glenn Cratty/Getty Images (Verbeek); Bill Wippert/NHLI/Getty Images (Gionta); David E. Klutho for Sports Illustrated (background)
Big Guys: Doug Pensinger/Getty Images (Chara); Denis Brodeur/NHLI/Getty Images (Beliveau); David E. Klutho for Sports Illustrated (background rink, Lemieux, Pronger); Steve Babineau/NHLI/Getty Images (Mahovlich); Bruce Bennett Studios/Getty Images (Gillies, Sundin); Robert Beck for Sports Illustrated (Thornton); Rick Stewart/NHLI/Getty Images (Lindros); Marianne Helm/Getty Images (Byfuglien)
Logos: Erick W. Rasco for Sports Illustrated (puck); David E. Klutho for Sports Illustrated (background)
Hardest Shots: Simon Bruty for Sports Illustrated (Chara); Paul J. Bereswill/Hockey Hall of Fame (Iafrate); John Russell/NHLI/Getty Images (Weber); David E. Klutho for Sports Illustrated (MacInnis); Bill Eppridge/Time & Life Pictures/Getty Images (Hull); Lou Capozzola for Sports Illustrated (Fedorov); David Bier Studios (Geoffrion); Andy Marlin/NHLI/Getty Images (Aucoin); Bob Rosato for Sports Illustrated (Stamkos); The Denver Post/Getty Images (Bathgate)
Overtime Games: Ray Lussier/Boston Herald American/AP (Orr); Gene J. Puskar/AP (sleeping in stands, Stars–Sabres); Tony Triolo for Sports Illustrated (Canadiens–Bruins); John Biever for Sports Illustrated (measuring stick)
Coaches: David E. Klutho for Sports Illustrated (Bowman, Babcock); B. Bennett/Getty Images (Blake, Adams); Denis Brodeur/NHLI/Getty Images (Arbour); Bruce Bennett Studios/Getty Images (Shero, Imlach); Doug Griffin/Toronto Star/Getty Images (Tarasov); Imperial Oil–Turofsky/Hockey Hall of Fame (Irvin); DK Photo/Getty Images (Sather)
Memorable Trades: Andrew D. Bernstein (Gretzky with sweater); Courtesy of The Edmonton Journal (Journal front page); Courtesy of The Edmonton Sun (Sun front page)
Goalies: B. Bennett/Getty Images (Roy); AP (Plante, Sawchuck, Hall); Gregory Shamus/NHLI/Getty Images (Brodeur); Denis Brodeur/NHLI/Getty Images (Hasek); Bruce Bennett Studios/Getty Images (Dryden, Parent); Melchior DiGiacomo/Getty Images (Tretiak); Mike Powell/Getty Images (Fuhr); David E. Klutho for Sports Illustrated (background)
Hair: Robert Laberge/Getty Images (Jagr); AP (Lafleur, Richard); Jim McIsaac/Getty Images (Commodore); Brad Watson/Getty Images (Melrose); Joel Auerbach/Getty Images (Kane); NHLI/Getty Images (Ricci); Steve Babineau/NHLI/Getty Images (Duguay); David E. Klutho for Sports Illustrated (Fraser); Bruce Bennett/Getty Images (Hartnell)
Non-NHL Games: Heinz Kluetmeier for Sports Illustrated (Miracle on Ice); Melchior DiGiacomo/Getty Images (Summit Series); Robert Beck for Sports Illustrated (2010 Olympic final); Denis Brodeur/NHLI/Getty Images (Super Series); B. Bennett/Getty Images (Canada Cup final); Jung Yeon-Je/AFP/Getty Images (2014 Olympic women's final); Richard Wolowicz/Getty Images (2009 World Junior semifinal, 2010 World Junior final); Rick Stewart/Getty Images (1996 World Cup final); David E. Klutho for Sports Illustrated (2009 NCAA Frozen Four final)
Nicknames: David E. Klutho for Sports Illustrated (Gretzky, Selanne); Denis Brodeur/NHLI/Getty Images (Howe); Bruce Bennett Studios/Getty Images (Richard, Vezina, Geoffrion); AP (Bobby Hull); Lou Capozzola for Sports Illustrated (Brett Hull); Vaughn Ridley/Getty Images (Cherry); Damian Strohmeyer for Sports Illustrated (Hasek)
Families: CP Picture Archive (Sutters); Richard Wolowicz/Getty Images (Brandon Sutter); Neil Leifer for Sports Illustrated (Howes); Denis Brodeur/NHLI/Getty Images (Dennis Hull, Danny Geoffrion); Al Bello/Getty Images (Brett Hull); AP (Bobby Hull); Hy Peskin for Sports Illustrated (Richards); Chris Seward/Raleigh News & Observer/MCT/Getty Images (Staals); Graig Abel/NHLI/Getty Images (Marc Staal); Bruce Bennett Studios/Getty Images (Phil Esposito, Syl Apps, Stastnys); Steve Babineau/NHLI/Getty Images (Tony Esposito, Syl Apps Jr.); Toby Talbot/AP (Syl Apps III); Harry How/Getty Images (Gillian Apps); Doug Pensinger/Getty Images (Yan Stastny); Bill Wippert/NHLI/Getty Images (Paul Stastny); Pictorial Parade/Getty Images (Morenz); CP/AP (Bernie Geoffrion); Joel Auerbach/Getty Images (Blake Geoffrion); David E. Klutho for Sports Illustrated (Granatos)
Captains: Linda Cataffo/NY Daily News Archive/Getty Images (Messier); David E. Klutho for Sports Illustrated (Yzerman, Lemieux, Gretzky, Sakic, Lidstrom); AP (Beliveau); Manny Millan for Sports Illustrated (Clarke); Bruce Bennett Studios/Getty Images (Potvin); Damian Strohmeyer for Sports Illustrated (Bourque)
Don Cherry Suits: (in numerical order) Rob Grabowski/USA Today Sports; Jim McIsaac/Getty Images (2); Kevin Light/NHLI/Getty Images; Andre Ringuette/NHLI/Getty Images; Leon T Switzer/Icon SMI; Dave Sandford/NHLI/Getty Images; Bruce Bennett/Getty Images; Dave Reginek/NHLI/Getty Images; Gerry Thomas/NHLI/Getty Images
Lines: B. Bennett/Getty Images (Production Line); Club de hockey Canadien Inc. (Punch Line); Bruce Bennett Studios/Getty Images (Lilco Line, KLM Line, Wayne's Line); Tony Triolo for Sports Illustrated (Dynasty Line); Peter Read Miller for Sports Illustrated (Triple Crown Line); Bill Sikes/AP (French Connection Line); AP (Kraut Line); Frank Lennon/Toronto Star/Getty Images (Espo Line); David E. Klutho for Sports Illustrated (background)
Players Who Never Won a Cup: George Long for Sports Illustrated (Dionne); Bruce Bennett Studios/Getty Images (Stastny); Robert Laberge/Getty Images (Oates); Denis Brodeur/NHLI/Getty Images (Hawerchuk); Steve Babineau/NHLI/Getty Images (Howe); Nevin Reid/Getty Images (Gartner); David E. Klutho for Sports Illustrated (Alfredsson, Joseph); Bob Rosato for Sports Illustrated (Sundin); Eric Schweikardt for Sports Illustrated (Park)
Shootout Artists: Robert Beck for Sports Illustrated (Oshie); Gregory Shamus/NHLI/Getty Images (Toews); Matt Slocum/AP (Nielsen); Dave Reginek/NHLI/Getty Images (Datsyuk); Ann Heisenfelt/AP (Parise); Minas Panagiotakis/Icon Sportswire/AP (Jokinen); Bill Wippert/NHLI/Getty Images (Boyes); Ross D. Franklin/AP (Vrbata); Mike Wulf/Cal Sport Media/AP (Christensen); Jonathan Daniel/Getty Images (Kane); redmal/Getty Images (background)
Goalie Masks: Heinz Kluetmeier for Sports Illustrated (Cheevers); Tony Triolo for Sports Illustrated (Cheevers's mask); Steve Babineau/NHLI/Getty Images (Gratton); Matthew Manor/Hockey Hall of Fame (Gratton's mask); Graig Abel Collection/Getty Images (Hayward); Bruce Bennett Studios/Getty Images (Hayward's mask, Bromley, Bromley's mask); David E. Klutho for Sports Illustrated (Quick, Miller); Michael Martin/NHLI/Getty Images (Quick's mask); Scott Levy/NHLI/Getty Images (Moog); Kent Hanson for Sports Illustrated (Moog's mask); Jonathan Nackstrand/AFP/Getty Images (Miller's mask); G Fiume/Getty Images (Hiller); Stephen Dunn/Getty Images (Hiller's mask); Doug Pensinger/NHLI/Getty Images (Richter); Ezra C. Shaw/Getty Images (Richter's mask); George Silk/The Life Picture Collection/Getty Images (Plante); Matthew Manor/Hockey Hall of Fame (Plante's mask)
Playoff Game 7s: Bruce Bennett/Getty Images (1994 Rangers); Jared Wickerham/Getty Images (2013 Bruins); Damian Strohmeyer for Sports Illustrated (2010 Flyers); David E. Klutho for Sports Illustrated (2014 Kings)
Terrible Sweaters: Glenn Cratty/Getty Images (Ducks, Islanders); Andre Ringuette/NHLI/Getty Images (Canadiens); David E. Klutho for Sports Illustrated (Stars); Bruce Bennett Studios/Getty Images (Canucks, Coyotes); Tim Smith/Getty Images (Oilers); Lou Capozzola for Sports Illustrated (Predators); Jim McIsaac/Getty Images (Lightning); Andre Ringuette/NHLI/Getty Images (Senators)
Dominant Teams: Dave Sandford/Hockey Hall of Fame (1976–77 Canadiens); AP (1975–76 Canadiens,1955–56 Canadiens, 1951–52 Red Wings, 1974–75 Flyers, engraving); Mike Ridewood/AP (1983–84 Oilers); Denis Brodeur/NHLI/Getty Images (1977–78 Canadiens); Neil Leifer for Sports Illustrated (1971–72 Bruins); David E. Klutho for Sports Illustrated (2014 Canadian Olympic team); Bruce Bennett Studios/Getty Images (1981–82 Islanders); B. Bennett/Getty Images (1985–86 CSKA)
Cup Day Stories: David E. Klutho for Sports Illustrated (Stanley Cup); Image Source/Getty Images (baby); Floortje/Getty Images (flower pot); Kapuk Dodds/Getty Images (Red Square); Kit Houghton/Dorling Kindersley/Getty Images (horse); ewg3D/Getty Images (road sign); Steve Gorton/Dorling Kindersley/Getty Images (screwdriver)
Untouchable Gretzky Records: Neil Leifer for Sports Illustrated